BOOKS BY JAY R. LEACH

How Should We Then Live
Behold the Man
The Blood Runs Through It
Drawn Away
Give Me Jesus
A Lamp unto My Feet
Grace that Saves
The Narrow Way
Radical Restoration in the Church
Manifestation of the True Children of God
According to Pattern
Battle Cry
Is there not a Cause?
We Would See Jesus
According to Pattern 2nd Edition
The Apostolic Rising
For His Glory

FOR HIS GLORY

THE CHURCH IS GOD'S GLORY
MADE VISIBLE TO THE WORLD

JAY LEACH

Order this book online at www.trafford.com
or email orders@trafford.com

Most Trafford titles are also available at major online book retailers.

Print information available on the last page.

ISBN: 978-1-6987-0622-1 (sc)
ISBN: 978-1-6987-0623-8 (e)

Scripture quotations marked NKJV are taken from the New King James Version.
Copyright © 1982 by Thomas Nelson, Inc. Used by permission. All rights reserved.

Scripture quotations are from the ESV® Bible (The Holy Bible, English
Standard Version®), copyright © 2001 by Crossway, a publishing ministry of
Good News Publishers. Used by permission. All rights reserved.

Scripture taken from The Holy Bible, King James Version. Public Domain

Scripture quotations marked NIV are taken from the Holy Bible, New International
Version®. NIV®. Copyright © 1973, 1978, 1984 by International Bible Society.
Used by permission of Zondervan. All rights reserved. [Biblica]

Trafford rev. 03/01/2021

Trafford
PUBLISHING®   www.trafford.com
North America & international
toll-free: 844-688-6899 (USA & Canada)
fax: 812 355 4082

CONTENTS

DEDICATION

Having been justified by faith, we have peace with God through our Lord Jesus Christ, through whom we have access by faith into this grace in which we stand and rejoice in hope of the glory of God. (Romans 5:1-2 NKJV)

But we all, with unveiled face, beholding as in a mirror the glory of the Lord, are being transformed into the same image from glory to glory, just as by the Spirit of the Lord. (2 Corinthians 3:18 ESV)

THE GREAT COMMANDMENT
AND THE GREAT COMMISSION

WHAT WE [THE CHURCH] ARE TO BE AND TO DO
[FOR HIS GLORY!]

"Love the Lord your God with all your heart and with all your soul and with all your mind ...... Love your neighbor as yourself. All the Law and the Prophets hang on these two commandments" (Matthew 22:37-40 ESV).

"Go and make disciples of all nations, baptizing them in the name of the Father and of the Son and of the Holy Spirit, and teaching them to obey everything I have commanded you" (Matthew 28:19-20 ESV).

"Go into all the world and preach the gospel to every creature" (Mark 16:15 ESV).

"As You sent Me into the world, I have also sent them ..." (John 17:18 ESV).

"You shall receive power after the Holy Spirit has come upon you" (Acts 1:8 ESV).

Why are we here? In Jesus' Scriptural response to that question every local church around the world is to be faithful and obedient to our Lord and Savior, and should focus all that we are and all that we do corporately and individually on the five-fold [equipping] purpose – that He gave us:

1. Love God
2. Love people
3. Go make disciples [win them]
4. Baptize them
5. Teach them to obey all that I have commanded

The enduring authority of Christ's commands should compel all Christians to study the Bible's teaching on the church. Proclaiming the Word makes the gospel audible – but Christians living together in local Christian communities make the Gospel visible (see John 13:34-35 ESV).

INTRODUCTION

"But we all with unveiled faces, beholding as in a mirror the glory of the Lord, are being transformed into the same image from glory to glory, just as by the Spirit of God" **(II Corinthians 3:18 ESV).**

Whether pursuing the Great Commission, witness-evangelism, or encouraging and edifying one another for Spiritual growth, through assembling for public praise, prayer and worship. One primary purpose prevails, the glory of God! Hopefully, at the same time, we are vigilant to make necessary changes in methods to remain relevant for changing people needs. While there are challenges, praise God, the manifold wisdom of God can be made known. This is accomplished in accordance with His eternal purposes of transforming true believers from glory to glory into the image of His Son. The Bible-centered local church is His unique instrument for bringing such glory to a postmodern society [world] gone wild. As we have closed the second decade of the twenty-first century, pastors and congregations would be wise to pause and take note of where they stand in conjunction with carrying out Christ's mandates: The Great Commandment and the Great Commissions to the glory of God. These are actual commands He gave to His church! No, not to a hierarchical few as is the case in the many local churches across this nation; but to all the members of His body, personally and corporately until He returns for His church. He also left instructions on how this is to be accomplished.

We witness daily the world as a sea of clashing beliefs. In such a fluid situation our feelings and circumstances constantly change; where can we find security? How can we expect to remain relevant without much prayer and restoration guidance from the Head of the church, Jesus Christ? The truth is, we can not find it, except through our Teacher, the Holy Spirit and God's Word working in tandem – in a restored Christ-centered local church. The Church of the Living God is a spiritual organism, in the world; but not of it! If not vigilant, the many religions and gods being introduced in this country through secularism, multiculturalism, natural religion, social media, public education and interaction with other deceptive means will profoundly affect congregations far and wide. Though reports show many people are accepting Christ as their Savior – churches *must* have in place spiritual formation strategies for these new converts. These new converts are extremely vulnerable to Satan's schemes designed to draw them into the many falsities expressed above. Again, if not properly spirit-formed and grounded on the true (life) foundation, Jesus Christ – their spiritual growth can be demonically arrested. Additionally, there is the radical theological diversity between Christian churches from regional mega-churches to the small storefronts, down the street and around the world. This include traditional churches [marked by static institutional ministry] and the Spirit-led churches [marked by the apostolic anointing, fruit of the Spirit, and gifts of the Spirit] that make up the true Christian experience today.

At every turn we find existing congregations struggling as they attempt to navigate their way in the present-day church scenes bogged-down in the old top-down hierarchal and institutional methodology of doing church [mostly the European influenced model]; which was prominent during earlier modern times. Therefore, many churches are knowingly or unknowingly assimilating secular humanistic adjustments from political correctness, tolerance, and conformity to the postmodern proponents of deconstruction, and extreme progressiveness or extreme conservatism. Approaching such hinderances without the power of the indwelling Holy Spirit (see Acts 1:8) and the Word of God leave those churches irrelevant to the people's spiritual needs. All rendering such local church no longer an effective counter-cultural. Much of what is considered church today is of human construct [Cain's variety]. Jesus said, "Without Me you can do nothing!"

Other local churches are adrift in the shifting currents of pragmatism. The rapidly-growing struggle stems from having been shaped mainly by the assumptions and challenges of the scientific/and rational approachs of modernism. As a result, many are ignorant of or simply ignoring the encroaching tenets of secular humanism [self and no God]. Then, there are those who through spiritual and biblical ignorance, willingly accept or allow opportunities for assimilation of this anti-God worldview.

The Spirit and the Word work in tandem within the faithful as keepers and guides in all areas of their lives. We are to remain true, vigilant and obedient to our Lord allowing His glory to shine in and through us in a anti-Christ culture and world.

The true apostolic Christian Church, the body of Christ, has stood both spiritually and biblically through a 2000 year history of effective ministry of the Great Commandments and the Great Commissions. That is to say, "God has a remnant of saints in every generation." This book is not about discrediting the local church nor the people of God. I love the church. My concern is the building up in love and obedience of the body of Christ for doing its Christ assigned missions in every generation. I believe in the local church, impowered and gifted for effective ministry by the Holy Spirit and a passionate faith in Jesus Christ's finished work on Calvary – that local church is still standing! We find the church challenged today by a radically changing time, the Greek *"anion"* refers to "a period of time."[1] Paul spoke of the "perilous times" to come in the last days: the great rejection of spiritual and biblical truth, due to growing acceptance of institutional religion seeking presenance over God and the things of God (see 2 Timothy 3:1-9).

From the very beginning of man's sin, just outside the gates of Eden two religions show up and have been running parallel with each other every since, both are identified in the sacrifices of Cain and Abel in Genesis 4. We see both practiced today in our local churches: Abel's *blood sacrifice* is characterized by what God requires. Cain's *bloodless sacrifice* is characterized by what humanity is willing to offer God. Vicious and dangerous describe the savage nature of people today as love for God, Christ and His Church wane and evil increases in the earth. Coping with the theological struggles produced through false beliefs, false gospels and new permissivism in worship forms of churches – demands that we remain faithful in our love for God and Christ in our prayers, our worship, our keeping biblical doctrine pure, and our urgent attentivness as God's Spirit-filled counter-cultural today!

Sadly, another most critical and challenging demand on the body of Christ today is the rejection of the priesthood of all believers – for a priesthood limited to a hierarchy of a faithful few produces mere spectators. Despite the priesthood of all believers, spiritually-gifted and operating in the biblical worldview developed through New Testament patterns and structures of spiritual organism is to the glory of God. His will is that *all* the people be fully-engaged in spiritual-growth [fruit] and service through the divine nature and the indwelling Holy Spirit.

Secularism promoted by "the spirit of the age," engages the culture to consider Christianity and the true spiritual biblical-based Christian Church to be exclusive, bigoted, outdated, irrelevant, alien, impenetrable, and by many too narrow and offensive. Additionally, always present within the ranks of the local churches are the challenges from a false religious Christianity characterized by the old pre-Reformation [1517] top-down hierarchal [organization model]. It is just another fleshy form focused on assimilating humanistic customs and traditions of by-gone generations; which clearly reject biblical truth and nullifies the moral law of God.

With seeking of the spiritual being, the in-thing today, many people are very agressively turning their attention from God and His grace to so-called inner spiritual New Age experiences. They become obsessed with angels, embrace eastern oriented religions, climb mountains, and other high places to appease their gods; while totally ignoring the *true* God, who created them. They travel to the ends of the earth fully devoted to seeking an understanding of "truth," but never encountering the One who is Truth and the Author of all truth, Jesus Christ.

They search the various cultures, religions, and philosophies of the world engaged in blending all kinds of worldly acts, rituals and counterfeit religious practices trying to find a path that reaches up to God – their

Creator but they are ignorant of the fact that He has already reached down to them through His risen Son, Jesus Christ, who abides in those who are His through the Promised Holy Spirit.

A survey of the Scriptures reveals that this was the challenge for the early Christian Church; as many Christians began to drift from the truth of God's Word; while struggling through tremendous persecution and hardships:

- Some began with the loss of the true gospel of Jesus Christ, salvation, and the New Covenant.
- Others seriously considered reverting back to the Law; while many did (Galatians 1:6 **ESV**).
- Eventually the Constantine era state-church *lost* the Holy Spirit, His gifts and ministries, and the character qualities of the early church along with the true gospel of Christ, true salvation, true forgiveness of sins, and true eternal life.
- The Roman Catholic church emerged as the depository of Christianity for the next eleven hundred years or until countered by the Reformation of 1517, spear-headed by a Catholic priest named Martin Luther.
- Presently, the United States and the West make up the depository of Christianity.

Secular humanism, multiculturism, extreme progressivism, extreme conservatism, and other ungodly cultural elements are constantly striving to influence the churches and sway many carnally-minded Christians to compromise and assimilate their agenda with its promotion of immoral elements. Their secular [no God] charges lodged against the Church and Christianity are that:

1. They have characterized evangelism [part of the churches' mission] as bigoted, antiquated, intolerant, and irrelevant.
2. They have determined portions of the Bible are hate speech; and in need of adjustment or replacement.
3. They promote their humanistic and atheistic initiatives against God, Christ, the Bible and Christians in general to insure their rapid removal from society and all public and governmental institutions.

While many churches continue to consider large buildings, programs, and numerical growth as the primary indicators of church health, secularism and atheism are chopping away all of the foundational truths of the Bible in this country. Not only have they practically anilated the institutions of marriage and the family, but through their open attack on Christianity, and the true gospel of Christ numbed the spiritual life out of many local churches. If this situation is not countered, *repentance, the gospel of Jesus Christ, forgiveness of sin, the new birth and eternal life will be compromised and soon lost!* The local churches must return to measuring success not in terms of numbers but through faithful obedience to the Lord's commands and a saving-knowledge of our Lord and Savior, Jesus Christ.

At the same time the church must choose resistance and be a counter-cultural or it will (silently) submit to a redefined cultural relevance; which bows to the everywhere-present worldly [societal] temptations. Their next step if not careful, will be their embracing a superficial spirituality that adapts the new progressivism, and natural religious Christianity, [full of works righteousness, half-truths, false faith and ethical respectability cast above Spirit and Truth]!

Living Christ's assigned mission to us means that we believe the Gospel of Jesus Christ is the answer to any question, circumstance, or failure life offers you – to God be the glory – for the great things He has done!

Angels, rituals, and human role models have their places. But the Holy Spirit's gospel message through us must be clear and unchanged; that none of these other things compare to Jesus Christ. And therein lies the power and promise of the gospel – Jesus Christ comes to us and offers Himself. Because He paid the ultimate price [shedding His precious blood] for our sins, we can now find the grace, mercy, forgiveness, peace and provision we so desperately need.

Remember, no matter how noble, cultured and learned you may be, the Scripture says, *"For all have sinned and fall short of the glory of God"* (Romans 3:23 NKJV). God has revealed His righteousness and how people are to live, but because of sin, no one can live up to what God created us to be – we *all* fall short of His glory.

It is the *experience* of the Spirit and biblical truth that deepens our [love] relationships with God and others.

Not only that, we can *experience* eternal life now, which Jesus Christ Himself describes as an intimate, never-ending love relationship with God the Father and God the Son.

My motivation for writing this book

1. To get the truth of the gospel of Christ into the hearts of all who will listen – while people who through voluntary spiritual and biblical illiteracy are trying to do the impossible.
2. To those who realize that any endeavor to live a Christian life without the empowerment of the Holy Spirit and the Word of God is impossible.
3. To warn and remind, that repentance is essential to turn from sin and receive God's forgiveness. Not only is repentance a personal matter, but can be exercised by groups and entire Christian communities.
4. To point out the pitfalls after having failed time and again, trying to work out the problems of life in our own strength – I have experienced failures and setbacks – walking in the flesh rather than walking in the Spirit, the results of years of self-actualization in the military, and yet I kept moving! A moving target is harder to hit. What about you?

Until I came into the knowledge of the truth and began to walk by faith in it – failure was inevitable. Specifically, this book is for those people who make up the congregations striving in [Romans 7 NKJV] to live a spiritual Christian life today. Is this where you find yourself? Prayerfully and carefully study chapters 1-8 of the Book of Romans, your breakthrough is sure! As stated earlier God has chosen to work through His people to bring about world redemption and spiritual awakening. From the outset, God has assured His people that repentance and obedience go together. Without obedience they would be destroyed (see Deuteronomy 30:16-15a NKJV). King Saul was a good example here – he rejected God's guidance. Notice the prophet Samuel spoke God's judgment to Saul (see 1 Samuel 13:13 NKJV).

A neutral approach

I have served as pastor of three traditional Baptist churches and one [organic church plant] – with several off-springs. I know that it is impossible to approach any subject from a neutral position, yet through the guidance of the Holy Spirit I will strive to do so in this book. While some of the things I say may step on your toes by describing your church, I didn't write specifically about your church.

I will take an objective stance to help others avoid the many pitfalls that hinder and sometimes block the Holy Spirit and His ministries from operating efficiently in the Christian community for the glory of God. It is my humble intention to address these issues from an objective stance to help others to be aware of the many pitfalls of walking in the flesh rather than the Spirit.

The Bible is my authority. Isn't it strange, the increasing questions faced by Christians concerning life in the local church, *and how they answer them differently?* Although they preach and teach the same gospel! How can this happen? What are we to think and do about such differences? This book contains my vision and hope for an apostolic restorative-model of church, apostolic methodology, and ministry based on every-member in spiritual organism. This model has been tried and tested, and some of which lie before me as a lifelong agenda.

It is my prayer that the message contained in the pages that follow will reach the heart of each reader in a most life-refreshment and change from glory to glory. It is with great expectation and glorious hope that together we can restore God's full truth and most important purpose, for His church, *"the glory of God!"*

In the Old Testament, God created a people for the glory of His name (see Exodus 9-12; Ezekiel 36:22-23 NKJV). The same is true in the New Testament. The church ultimately exists for His glory. Whether pursuing missions, encouraging growth in holiness; and assembling for public praise, prayer, worship and instruction, this one purpose prevails. The church is the unique instrument for bringing God such glory (Hebrews 10:25 NKJV).

Accordingly, God's intent "is that the manifold wisdom of God be made known to the rulers and authorities in the heavenly realms, according to His eternal purpose which he accomplished in Christ Jesus our Lord" (Ephesians 3:10-11 NKJV).

Christ's work continues in the church, that is the fullness of the mystery of God in redemption disclosed among His people. The church arises only from the gospel. A distorted church is usually derived from a distorted gospel! May we ever be "as living stones being built up into a spiritual house, a holy priesthood to offer up spiritual sacrifices acceptable to God through Jesus Christ" (1 Peter 2:5 NKJV).

In the light of this Scripture, as true Christians we are New Testament believer-priests[2] and ministers of reconciliation living and practicing the life of righteousness imputed and holiness imparted to us by our wonderful Lord and Savior, Jesus Christ! God is looking for a holy people through whom He can work in revealing Himself to a fearful watching world. God needs clean vessels. Today more than ever, God wants people, families, and local churches who will obey and serve Him. This is my prayer – for His glory. In John 7:38, Christ promised that, "He who believes in Me, as the Scriptures have said; out of his heart will flow rivers of living water." "Is that you friend?"

Jay R. Leach

Fayetteville, North Carolina

SECTION I

THE CHALLENGE

CHAPTER ONE

RELEVANCE: A GOOD STRATEGY?

"Rejoice with those who rejoice, and weep with those who weep" (Romans 12:15 NKJV).

I have noticed through the years that when local churches reach out to the people and families in their sphere of influence by helping to meet physical as well as spiritual needs; and be there for people in crisis, they win their trust and draw them to the Savior, Jesus Christ. One example comes to my mind among the many like opportunities caused by the climatic conditions we are all experiencing across America, a family was in dire need as the father, the family's sole income provider, suffered a long bed-ridden hospital stay.

A local church stepped in to help them with several delinquent mortgage payments and other necessities in Jesus' name. The family was unchurched; but when the husband regained his health and strength the family came to thank the church for their love and generosity – they accepted Christ and became a part of the Christian Community.

1

Today, a couple of generations later that family and church are still there carrying on, witnessing, and meeting needs of the world around them. Undoubtedly, this church follows the Lord's mandate to make disciples.

Consider the present world-wide COVID-19 pandemic, wherein every local church has ample opportunities to generously sow and to reap. There was a time when the local church was at the center of the local community. A church then, operating from the perspective, of relevance provided a great strategy for relevant ministry and that potential remains for many local churches. How? According to Webster's Dictionary that church is relevant as it has "significant and demonstrable bearing on the matter at hand." So, the opposite is equally true, answering questions no one is asking; and offering solutions that do not meet obvious needs is deemed irrelevant; which equates to the church or the individual Christian actually doing little or nothing.

The gospel is the answer to every need

People are not attending church gatherings as in years past, not even the traditional Christmas and Easter events. Many people think anything, we may have to say or offer as Christians is irrelevant to the deep needs haunting their lives. This is increasingly true with the unchurched and a growing number of the churched, especially the young adults. Many of them have determined that they get better results from social media and other world systems.

A major cause of this dilemma is the lax in Bible study in the home as well as the church today, false teachings, and voluntary biblical illiteracy have infiltrated the local churches resulting in many half-truths by heirlings rather than the truthful preaching and teaching of the whole counsel of God. Then there are many hard-working pastors suffering from burn-out, Why? Because they are trying to do it all alone, God forbid! Next, there are many like Hollywood who *feel* that they must delete much of the truth of God's Word to make it palatable and insert untruths to make it entertaining. I cringe at some of the so-called fitting tributes and eulogies paid to the deceased today such as "he or she always made me laugh." "He or she is up there smiling down on us." Every time I hear such comments, I think of the access baggage [such as loneliness, fear, and despair] this person is carrying around that causes them to seek such superficial joy. No wonder "Universalism" has become so popular. No one is going to hell anymore, because according to this false religious belief all are going to heaven anyway, so be happy! These lies certainly helps to explain the lack of Bible study and prayerlessness marking many churches today.

Others charge that local churches are again, answering questions that no one is asking; and suggesting solutions to problems the people are not facing. We are irrelevant to those we need to reach the most! They leave our services feeling just as alone and hopeless as they did when they came in. Such churches are like those doctors who treat the symptoms hoping that maybe one day we'll get to the root of the problem. As a result, much of what is offered may soothe us for a little while, but the old malady is still there.

It is estimated that more than 50% of people going to the doctors are seeking physical solutions for spiritual problems. Though the human secularists and atheists are a grave threat not to be ignored; another perhaps even greater threat is forfeiture of a vital relationship with God and His Word to a culture of marketing, programs, entertainment, and left and right-wing partisan politics. The larger concern here is those people who identify themselves as Christians but show absolutely no evidence of the biblically held beliefs that have historically marked true Christianity.

The true gospel of Jesus Christ is the solution to mankind's deepest needs. God and His eternal Word are ultimately relevant to the needs of every culture, even ours; but on His term not ours. So, the irrelevancy between us and the world around us is not God's fault. Somewhere between God's ultimate answers to their problems – His message of hope is being improperly transmitted by us, His ministers of reconciliation (see 1 Corinthians 15:1-5; 2 Corinthians 5:18).

The fallacy is not in the message; but in the messengers. Most people just can't grasp how God and His Word can possibly solve their struggles in life and sadly, [a growing number of them are church members who attend on a [regular basis]. Other realities include: the high rate of pastor turnover, depression, and the resignation rates of pastoral ministry. All could be attributed to the insistence on top-down leadership wherein the sole authority lies with the pastor of the church. But is this how the Bible distributes authority in the local church? The pastor does the work of the church while the members go about their own business and doing their own thing?

"Every member in ministry," [spiritual organism] of the New Testament removes the perception that the church belongs to the pastor and that only the elite can enter the Lord's service.

I do not know of a denomination or a local church in existence that has as its goal to "teach its people to do all that Jesus commanded."
– Dallas Willard

Only the ministry elite [top down] is prevalent in [institutional ministry]; which is the traditional model of doing church. In this model of ministry, many times because of accessive programing, the Holy Spirit is hindered or denied to the point there is really no place for Him nor His gifts and Ministries! So, in these cases we find ethical respectability acceptable in lieu of the salvation experience. Because these churches stand for nothing – today they are falling for anything. Only God's grace to a Spirit-filled, Bible believing church can reap a wonderful harvest of souls!

Shared or body leadership [spiritual organism] creates room for the operation of diverse Spiritual gifts and graces. Even in churches with shared leadership, at times people tire beneath the heavy load of pastoral ministry. While spiritual organism or body ministry requires some organization such as [servant] leadership, the ministry remains bottom up rather than top down. I used to wonder how a pastor could maintain such a busy schedule of:

- Committee meetings
- Board meetings
- Civic meetings
- Pastoral visitation
- Church services and other clerical duties
- Community and other demands

When I entered the ministry I quickly found out. Without help there's only so much the best pastors can do. Because of the heiracial model of church, our pastor was sometimes forced to neglect some of the more important matters of ministry:

- Prayer
- Study
- Teaching

Team Ministry

Having more spiritual and biblically *qualified* people serve with him would have made the ministry more effective and much more joyful. Because we have a mission, we organize, and mobilize to accomplish that which we have been assigned to do. We appoint leaders and organize our people according to their giftedness and callings. We review opportunities, put together resources, and engage a strategy that will enable us to challenge the established values in our world and allow us to begin the process of restoration and reconciliation that God desires.

Of course, this is all in vain if we remain within the four walls of our homes and churches talking about going – but when we are [*all*] equipped to deploy, equipped to expand the kingdom (see 2 Timothy 2:2 NKJV) for:

- We demolish arguments and pull down every pretension that sets itself up against the knowledge of God and take captive every thought to be obedient to Christ (2 Corinthians 10:5).
- We *all* deploy into our world, neighborhoods, schools, workplaces, cities and towns displaying *this new way of thinking and living, [spiritual organism]*.
- We speak of the good news that through Christ sins can be forgiven and; the kingdom of God is available to all.
- We comfort the sick, feed the hungry, care for the poor, and stand up for justice.
- We live and lead with love in our hearts and truth on our lips, gaining respect and trust, winning people to Christ and inspiring hope.

All must go

One wonders why more churches don't share authority among qualified ordained and un-ordained ministers. If we are going to restore the church [spiritual organism], body ministry, no longer can we allow:

- Fear over faith
- Fear of change
- Fear of men [backstabbing]
- Possessive leadership
- Idolatrous attachment to "the pastor"
- Lack of biblical knowledge
- Denial of the Holy Spirit's gifts and ministries
- Denial of the Great Commandment and the Great Commission

Neither can we allow a perceived lack of qualified people to hinder the sharing of biblical leadership in the church. Of course, it's necessary that we sketch a few points concerning the proper exercise of leadership in the church:

- First and foremost, it must be clearly understood that *all authority is derived from Christ.* Authority is not inherited; it is delegated.
- In the church, only Jesus' authority is underived. In the church Jesus Christ is the only and sufficient HEAD of the church.
- In the church, authority must be mingled with love [agape] and fellowship [koinonia] serving the well-being of *[all]* those under our care as we must give account. Christ is our greatest Example (see Hebrews 13:17; Mark 10:45; Colossians 3:23 NKJV).
- The Bible requires the entire church to submit to the entire leadership. This is very important because abusive situations usually include individual leaders taking advantage of individual members. Biblical authority does not work that way. In apostolic ministry, all members grow in wisdom and knowledge as they benefit from the collective team around them.

What many local traditional churches need is a real live-model demonstration. On military Installations from time to time the military puts on live fire demonstrations for the local civilian populace – when the big guns go off, you can hear, "WOW!"

Our neighbors are desperate to see the Word of God proclaimed with a demonstration of God's presence and power applied to the lives and real needs of the people. God gave us the ultimate example in Jesus Christ on how to be a showcase of God's glory. The Apostle John says,

"But if we walk in the light as He is in the light, we have fellowship with one another, and the blood of Jesus Christ His Son cleanses us from all sin" (1 John 1:7 NKJV).

The kind of showcase we are to be, must begin with Jesus' timeless words to Nicodemus, a prominent ruling member of the Jewish council. After having looked at Jesus closely; his thoughts about Him were:

1. "You are a teacher come from God!"
2. "No man can do these miracles that you do *except* God be with Him."
3. His conclusion of the matter was, "You *are* God come down from heaven to teach us!" "WOW!" Emphasis added.

Jesus answered, *"Verily, verily"* as if to say, Nicodemus, "What I am about to say to you is *eternally important."* It is so important that it's impossible for you to *see* the kingdom of God without it. Despite many high-profile people whose views declare many ways to God! "There is no other way, Nicodemus!"

"Except a man be born again, he cannot see the kingdom of God" (John 3:3). Except you repent, you shall likewise perish! Emphasis added.

The *necessity* of the new birth grows out of the "impossibility" of the natural man to "see" or "enter into" the kingdom of God. Nicodemus thought Jesus meant that he would have to be physically born again (v. 4, 9). Jesus made it clearly *personal* for Nicodemus and for you and me. The new birth *is not* a reformation of our old nature (see Romans 6:6), but a *creative act* of the Holy Spirit: *"a new man"* (Carefully and prayerfully study John 3:5; 1:12, 113; II Corinthians 5:17; Ephesians 2:10 NKJV).

A new creation

The new man is the regenerate person as distinguished from the *old man* of (Romans 6:6) and is a new man – having become partakers of the divine nature and life.

"By great and precious promises, that through these you may be partakers of the divine nature having escaped the corruption that is in the world through lust" (2 Peter 1:4 NKJV). Emphasis added.

"For you died, and your life is hidden with Christ in God. When Christ who is our life appears, then you also will appear with Him in glory" (Colossians 3:3, 4 NKJV).

"Do not lie to one another, since you have put off the old man with his deeds and have put on the new man who is renewed in knowledge according to the image of Him who created him" (Colossians 3:9, 10 NKJV).

In verses 9 and 10, Paul uses analogies between the *old man* and our old sinful lives and the *new man* and our *new lives in* Jesus Christ! He parallels his discussion in Romans 6 about *dying to sin* and living for Christ. It is important to note that his references to the words "old man" and "new man" do not refer to the Christian's *fleshly* and *spiritual natures*. The old man is under and old master, Satan, while the new man has a new master, the Spirit of Christ living in him. Jesus said, *"...... without Me you can do nothing ..."* (John 15:5).

This Word from the Lord should alert all Christians individually and corporately that to divorce the Holy Spirit or leave Him out of their lives means that at best you are carnally-minded and operating in the flesh:

- The flesh sets its desires *against* the Spirit, and the Spirit *against* the flesh; for these are in opposition to one another (see Galatians 5:17 NKJV).
- The fruit of man is greed, power, corruption, and control; while believers filled with the Holy Spirit see things from a heavenly perspective and can easily discern works of the flesh:

  "Now the works of the flesh are evident, which are adultery, fornication, uncleanness, lewdness, idolatry, sorcery, hatred, contentions, jealousies, outbursts of wrath, selfish ambitions, dissensions, heresies, envy, murders, drunkenness, revelries, and the like; of which I tell you beforehand, just as I also told you in time past, that those who practice such things will not inherit the kingdom of God" (see Galatians 5:19-24).

- This is disobedience; since the Scripture commands us, "Do not walk according to the flesh, but walk according to the Spirit" (see Romans 8:1 NKJV).

I think we are experiencing a doctrinal divide in many Christian churches in America today, no matter the denominational persuasion. The authority and integrity of Scripture is not a frequent teaching. In fact, the teaching of basic biblical Christian doctrine is no longer a priority in many local churches. Again, human secularism [self and no God] has become the norm in public education today while Christianity has been snubbed or totally rejected as non-essential.

A new man

The necessity of being "born again from above" is absent or watered-down along with the preaching of the true gospel of Jesus Christ in many local churches. The full *truth in salvation* is the difference between the old man [*born once*, natural birth] and the new man, *born twice*, [natural birth and spiritual birth from above].

We must all acknowledge the preciousness of the true gospel of Jesus Christ (1 Corinthians 15:1-5)! Church history speaks of eleven hundred years wherein the true gospel and eternal life were lost to the people. The Scripture declares, "It is the power of God unto salvation" (Romans 1:16).

How could one ever become a Christian in an atmosphere
in which the pure gospel is rarely if ever preached?
– R. T. Kendall

As more and more churches substitute institutional religion [institutionalism] for the true spiritual and biblical Christianity, many congregations with a lack of sanctified influencers are organizing around worldly influenced ministry models for management and accounting purposes; which becomes the end rather than the means to an end. Additionally, people are being received into membership without the new birth with the hope; they will eventually experience it:

- Many people operate in the local churches clearly based on their natural talents, rather than Spiritual gifts.
- With others once their names are on the rolls it just doesn't seem to matter?
- Having people working in the church while engaging in questionable or sinful lifestyles are becoming the norm for many congregations.

Eden revisited

Satan has been successful with his deception of secular humanism – a belief system that began as a religion, but after many years, withdrew that claim in order to fully engage their secular agenda without the restraints of religion. Secularism's diabolical goal is to wipe-out God, Christ, Christians and all the things of God. Notice their gains so far during the COVID-19 epedemic – eliminating the church as non essential. Through this deception, Satan is systematically neutralizing all of the public square concerning *absolutes* and *truth* through the great lie, [extreme permissivism] "no absolutes." They have been very successful because the Bible teaches that the social structure of this world is controlled by a prevailing principle of life that is foreign to God and leads people away from Him. This principle was at work in Eden and has penetrated federal and local governments, the courts, public education at all levels, and other public institutions to include many churches and any other components that makes up society. Who would dream that an individual after openly inciting fringe groups to boast of taking over the Capital with the intention of overthrowing the U.S. Government for personal gains could still be receiving "morning breafings" [self-exclamitory] from that Government? Why should any faction "of the people" have to fear his return to the nations's highest office? In other words, the same vulnerable weaknesses that the devil explored in man in the Garden of Eden, continue to be one of his chief weapons today. As the prince of this world's (systems), Satan uses the *material world,* the *people of the world,* and the *value systems of the world.* Statistics confirm that the people of America have become the most immoral people in the world, who boasts, "if you can get away with it – it must be right." Earlier I said, "this nation is the present depository of Christianity and the world's greatest center for Christian teaching." That may be hard for some to understand, but the fact is many Christians are not living by the moral standards taught in the Bible. Our society has been exalted far above all other societies giving it great power in all areas of worldly influence to *tempt* and try to *deceive* Christians so that we will *become independent and step outside of God's Word.* He used the same satanic tactics that brought down Adam and Eve [disobedience], today the commandment is Hebrews 10:25), notice:

The Lord God planted a garden eastward in Eden, and there He put the man whom He had formed. And out of the ground the Lord God made every tree grow that is pleasant to the sight and good for food. The tree of life was in the midst of the garden, and the tree of the knowledge of good and evil (Genesis 2:8, 9 NKJV).

Then the Lord God took the man and put him in the garden of Eden to tend and keep it. And the Lord God commanded the man saying, "Of every tree of the garden you may eat freely; **but of the tree of the knowledge of good and evil "you shall not eat, for in the day that you eat of it, you shall you shall surely die"** *(Genesis 2:15-17 NKJV). Emphasis added.*

Satan's goal was to control Eve's thoughts and actions. We see this clearly when Satan tempted and deceived her:

When the woman saw that the fruit of the tree was good for food (lust of the flesh), *and pleasing to the eye* (lust of the eye), *and also desirable for gaining wisdom* (pride of life), *she took some and ate it* (Genesis 3:6).

Then the Lord God said to the woman, "What is this you have done?" The woman said, "The serpent (Satan) *deceived me, and I ate"* (Genesis 3:13).

The Scriptures teach that the deception we face daily springing from the world systems are the same three; which together make up our old *unconvertable* sinful nature:

1. *The lust of the flesh*
2. *The lust of the eye*
3. *The pride of life*

- Secularism accepts anything or any view in which human interests dominate; man is god and promotes **"self."**

- Secularism emphasizes reason, science, and human fulfillment – at the same time rejecting the existence of God or the importance of Christianity.
- Secularism promotes moral relativism and denies there is a right and wrong; totally discounting the Bible. The idea being to move Christians away from obeying the Word of God.
- Secularism's worldview directly conflicts with the biblical Christian worldview.
- Secularism believes that man is the center of all things – therefore in this view the mind of man is the center of reality.
- Secularism has publically made known their desire to remove God, Christ, the church and all Christians from the public square.

The secular influences in our culture seem to search us out. Their now strong forces captivate people daily. Sadly, many Christians try to assimilate tenets from their humanistic agenda with biblical Christianity. But if God is Creator, if Jesus Christ is the only Way, and if the Bible is true and it is; humanism is a disastrous deception; accepted by our culture as a norm, but not without many casualties.

Wherever you go even among some Christians, the things of the world will trump the conversation. Humanism and atheism very subtly dominate much of public opinion, all levels of education, social media and a lot of so-called Christian counseling and Christian education today. The powerful influence of our society has caused many Christians to *place a greater emphasis on* supplying their <u>physical needs</u> and <u>wants</u> of their families than in *supplying their <u>spiritual needs.</u>* Never before has the *Christian family* felt the pressure and power of *worldly society* to *conform to its ways.* Life is totally meaningless, if our ancestors were monkeys, apes, or life evolved from nothing. Evolution [theory] is spoken of as truth and Creation as false. Some even consider themselves theistic evolutionists?

We are rapidly becoming a numbed society; as talk therapy succumbs to drug therapy associated with all manmade cures. In many quarters, depression, despair, and even suicide – today are considered the norm. Much of the local churches' counsel today [begins with man rather than the true Source, God], as we become more humanistic like the worldly culture.

Many of these churches' mission statements says, "belong and believe" rather than "believe and belong." In either case *until* we repent and turn back to God in obedience, the biblical experience of the new birth from above, and living a life of holiness – remains on a slippery sloop:

- Many people remain unregenerate in our churches.
- The Holy Spirit is not their guide.
- Christ is not in them and they are not "in Him"
- Until a covenant relationship is established through the shed blood of Jesus Christ; the middle wall of separation remains in place for them.

Salvation never originates in the efforts of people; it always arises out of the loving-kindness of God. The essential truth is "salvation is of the Lord" (Jonah 2:9 NKJV).

No matter how talented, moral, or refined; the natural person may be; he or she is blind to spiritual truth and cannot enter the kingdom of God; neither can he or she understand, obey, please and glorify God. The new birth is not a reformation of the old nature, but a regeneration! In this age of voluntary biblical illiteracy and ignorance, it is imperative that we ensure our own foundation is established on the correct doctrines of Jesus Christ and His atoning sacrifice. The cross of Jesus Christ has shattered all of our hope in the things that the world has to offer.

A new heart

Jesus Christ now lives in the new man because the "I" has personally experienced the new birth from above by the Spirit. Remember it's not what we do for God, but what God does for us, when we believe in His Son. In Ezekiel 36:26: God said,*"I will give you a new heart and put a new spirit within you."* The heart is the seat of affection. In regeneration [which is not really regeneration], without repentance – God spiritually gives us a new heart with:

- A new purpose for living
- A new potential
- A new personality
- A new family

- A new destiny
- A new love, peace and joy [in the Holy Spirit]

"O What a wonderful change in my life has been wrought since Jesus came into my heart!"

Paul gives the Colossians instructions for proper conduct which are just as applicable for the body of Christ today. Put to death in your members those sinful things which are of the earth:

- Fornication
- All uncleanness
- Evil passions
- Evil desire
- Covetousness
- Idolatry

Because of these things the wrath of God is coming upon the sons of disobedience, in which you yourselves once walked when you lived in them, but now you yourselves are to put off all of these (see Colossians 3:3-10):

- Anger
- Wrath
- Malice
- Blasphemy
- Filthy language
- Do not lie

A new spirit

As the elect of God, holy and beloved, put on tender mercies:

- Kindness
- Humility
- Meekness
- Long suffering
- Bearing with one another
- Forgiving one another

If anyone has a complaint against another; even as Christ forgave you, so you also must do. But above all these things, put on love which is the bond of perfection [maturity]. In Colossians 3:16-17 NKJV, Paul sums up the whole matter of how Christians should live, "Let the words of Christ dwell in you richly in all wisdom, teaching and admonishing one another in psalms and hymns and spiritual songs, singing with grace in your hearts to the Lord. And whatever you do in word and deed, do all in the name of the Lord Jesus Christ, giving thanks to God the Father through Him." We should put on the character of the "new Man" and commit everything we do or say to Jesus and continually thank God for all His good gifts.

Salt and Light

Our righteously-lived lives must be such [salt and light] that they prompt the watching world to want what we have as they exclaim, "GOD IS AWESOME!" The world is full of fearful, hurting and needy people, just like the family we mentioned in the beginning of the chapter. Believe me we are just scratching the surface. The general population can be characterized as people who are:

- Fearful – of what they are seeing in the natural without hope [the many losses due to the COVID-19: i.e. church, deaths, home, and employment].
- Alienated – (from God and His Word)
- Disconnected – (from one another)
- Alone – (feeling empty, and unloved)

Research shows that hurting people may often times come to the right place [church], but often many go away sad and empty because the way we answer their questions do not relate to their growing needs. A great part of this aggravation can be traced to a lie that many are aware of in the local church but will not address. Therefore, its presence simply furthers the misunderstanding through the increase of carnal Christians on the inside of the church; who are in more conformity with the tenets of secularism on the outside.

Satan is happy each time they achieve a victory. Their form of a natural-religious Christianity promotes a secular progressive agenda which supports separation of the so-called sacred and the secular. In God's Word, there is no distinction between the sacred and the secular for the Christian. All belong to God!

The secular/ sacred entrapment

One of the most glaring hindrances toward the Christian's full participation in the plan of God is – the passed down habit of separating the sacred[3] and the secular.[4] When these two are erroneously perceived most people think that the two:

- Exist separate from each other.
- Are morally and spiritually incompatible.
- Yet, we cross back and forth out of necessity from one to the other daily.

For many their inner man has adapted to the situation as normal or "that's all there is;" so, they live a divided life instead of a unified one. What complicates the situation, as Christians we inhabit two worlds – the spiritual and the natural.

Natural

However, before we were born again; as Satan's children we lived our lives on earth in the natural, and subject to the limitations of the flesh and the weaknesses of our inherited sinful nature from Adam. We experienced much hard work and attention to the things of this world.

Spiritual

In contrast to the natural, as the children of God we are by position in Christ in heaven enjoying an intimate relationship with Him. But bodily we are still here on the earth [His salt and light] bringing flavor and reflecting His glory to counter the darkness of the world. Therefore, we find ourselves in a dilemma; every act we experience will be either secular or sacred; that is according to the world's thinking and labeling.

The spiritual normally include our daily holy habits of Bible reading, prayer, singing and church attendance. Through these acts we relate to the spiritual; we go out to our places of employment, recreation, buy groceries, doctor appointments and many other activities that we share with the so-called secular culture are labeled secular [without God]; if not careful we could try to imitate their actions, conduct and identity.

Think about it, the secular includes all the ordinary acts of daily life that we share with all humans: eating, sleeping, shopping, going to work, [we call it our secular job], looking after our physical needs and other routine duties. Most Christians are caught up trying to satisfactorily adjust to the demands of both. I read that Evangelist Billy Graham's wife had a sign over the sink in the kitchen and noted that she worshipped [washing dishes] there three time a day.

This whole situation is like the theory of evolution; which states that various kinds of plants, animals, and humans descended from other kinds that lived in earlier times.[5] Christendom is defined as, the place where the Church is located;[6] which is another man-made theoretical concept.

These unbiblical theories are simply smokescreens and deceptions activated by Satan, who "transforms himself into an angel of light. Therefore it is no great thing if his ministers also transform themselves into ministers of righteousness....." (2 Corinthians 11:14-15). They strive to divert the Christian's attention from what matters most, *truth*, and living an obedient and righteous Christian life for the glory of God. Neither of the three concepts mentioned above have a foundation or place in true Christianity.

Peace and **Deliverance** from this dilemma for the New Testament believer-priests come only through understanding and taking appropriate obedient practical action on the revealed truth of God's Word.

All belongs to God

The Lord Jesus Christ is our perfect example, and with Him there was no such thing as this hindrance of trying to walk the tightrope of a divided life. God accepted the offering of Jesus Christ's total life; making no distinction between anything He did – and now our lives must be the same. He ate with sinners, as well as the righteous. Jesus said, "I do always those things that please Him" (John 8:29). Jesus never suffered or experienced the pressures of moral or spiritual uncertainty.

Paul exhorts all believers to *"do all to the glory of God"* which introduces the understanding that the Christian's vocation is service and worship unto God. All acts are worship contributing to the glory of God. True worship begins by realizing that God seeks those who worship Him with all of who they are!

Paul did not move up to some pious act for example but used simple acts of eating and drinking; as if he was looking down through the corridors of time to today where eating and drinking is such a public activity and unless we are ashamed to do so – we can honor God not for any outside show, but our giving thanks for our meals which is an act of worship to our God.

The true New Testament believers are living according to the will of God as revealed to them by the Spirit and the Word of God. Carnality in the church is due largely to a lack of engagement with the Spirit and the Word. Both are being ignored, yet many claim to have a knowing relationship with God without either. Herein lies the *division* of the acts. This brings no act as some may think down to human level, but it lifts every act up to the heavenly kingdom of God to His glory. We should view the total of all we are and do every day as acts of worship, no exceptions. When I am preaching, teaching, writing a book or cutting the grass, all are worship – the Father wants me to worship Him in these and all other acts to His glory.

The same is true in your life. God wants you to view *everything* as an act of worship. In Job 1:20-21, we see that even enduring hardships offer us an opportunity for worship – notice Job's response! It's possible for us to worship in a hospital bed, and even in a financial crisis. Many positive testimonies to the glory of God have come forth over the past decade from shootings, accidents, hurricanes, tornados, fires, earthquakes and certainly COVID-19. Yet, we are witnessing many Christians still praising and worshipping God in spite of all the pain and devastation. People continue to acknowledge His rich mercies toward them even though many of them will never be able to return to their homes again! The Word of God says, *"And we know that all things work together for good to those who love God, to those who are the called according to His purpose"* (Romans 8:28). Give Him praise and glory!

Living a righteous life of obedience and sprinkling the blood of Jesus Christ in [in every act] is worship (see 1 Peter 1:2). Lest we forget in the exercise of our office as New Testament believer-priests we are worshippers who offer a threefold sacrifice in everything to our God:

1. The individual's own living body (see Romans 12:1; Philippians 2:17; 2 Timothy 4:6; 1 John 3:16; James 1:27).
2. The individual's own praise to God, "the fruit of the lips offered in His name" continually (see Hebrews 13:15; Exodus 25:22).
3. The individual's substance (see Hebrews 13:16; Romans 12:13; Galatians 6:6, 10; III John 5-8; Hebrews 13:2; Titus 3:14).

Additionally, as N.T. believer-priests we are to give ourselves wholly to the priestly work of intercession. In Colossians 4:12 NKJV, Paul writes, *"…. Always laboring fervently for you in prayers that you may stand perfect and complete in all the will of God."*

Our daily walk: a Sacrament

I am fascinated with the way Paul engaged in transitioning from the "gospel" and "resurrection chapter," (1 Corinthians 15) right into the collection, "our giving and offerings" in the 16th chapter. In many of our local churches the offering is considered secular [public] even to the point that many times carnally-minded people are appointed to do this work.

These are by choice carnally-minded people over the treasury and other earthly properties. Sometimes using various schemes including begging to get more, even twisting the truth of God's Word to make it fit man-made promises. Paul's instructions say simply "lay aside as you prosper" indicating that our giving is *an act of worship.*

Many Christians' attitude toward giving to the Lord's work is like an illustration I read wherein a twenty-dollar bill ran into a one-dollar bill on the street one day. The dollar delightfully asked the twenty where he had been so long, the twenty said, "O," I've been in the fabulous casinos and luxurious hotels on the French Rivera, Los Vegas, Atlantic City and numerous luxury cruises." By the way, "Where have you been?" The one-dollar bill shamefully replied, "Church!"

The knowledge that believers are in right relationship with God the Father and one another through our saving relationship in Jesus Christ the Son; the Holy Spirit will unify our individual lives and at the same time bring us to the point of making *everything* sacred to us. Seeing the truth of this matter is not enough alone. We must be delivered from this dilemma if we are to have complete peace.

We must *practice* living for the glory of God (prayerfully study Romans 7-12). Old habits die hard. Consider the following:

- The average Christian will have a problem grasping the ideal that his or her daily employment (job) can and should be performed as an act of worship for the glory of God.
- The devil will never be happy with your leaving him for Christ. He huffs and puffs like the big bad wolf, of the "fairy tale," but you just remember the promise of God – "no weapon formed against you shall prosper." This holds true with tyrant employers who dislike you because you are a Christian [salt and light], but won't dare fire you, because you do the job with excellence and integrity as an act of Worship.
- I personally experienced that on several of my many assignments in the military. I also experienced that in my uniqueness as a Christian in the military, God is gracious and rewards obedience. God gave me favor with the Chain of Command from Privates to General officers. Many donot feel comfortable around you, but over time even your enemy will bow to Christ within you; and I assure you your prayer life and spiritual growth will be meteoric.
- Take heart and stand by faith on the presence and promises of Almighty God – who exhorts us not to fear the one who can kill the body – but fear Him who is able to destroy soul and body!

We walk by faith

Lest we forget that the walk of all believers from Abel in the O.T. (see Genesis 4:4; Hebrews 11:4 NKJV) to our total walk as ministers of reconciliation is "by faith" and not "by sight." So, we must aggressively hold firm our position and "just know" that every thought and act of every hour 24/7 is included in our acts toward God. We are a remnant – not a crowd.

In our times of private prayer, we must bring to God our commitment that we mean every act for His glory – then we must supplement those times of prayer with meditation in the truth of God's Word and keep our minds on things above. This lifestyle is for our entire life-time. At some point we all have no doubt fallen short but remember our instructions for falling short are found in (1 John 1:7, 9).

One of Satan's on going strategies is to silence believers in the public square. For now, he influences local churches to agree that the proper *way* of worship is to silently privatize all expressions of our faith in public. Therefore, he is saying everywhere else is his territory, [secular] places, and things are – "off limits" to all Christians except those who make the necessary adjustments to tolerate [agree] with their progressive secular worldviews; beginning with the rejection of God, Christ and the things of God which have no place in a progressive society. Just one of many examples to emphasize the point: a college professor was fired because he refused to remove his Bible from his classroom desktop. His Bible had been there many years for use in his his daily devotions.

The enemy in high earthly places is making inroads with these and other deceptions through doubt, unbelief, complexes, sympathy and support of those considered by them to be the down-trodden. They harass Christians with lies, accusations of bigotry, and fanaticism – all with the endorsement of Hollywood, social media, and political correctness, and they are getting away with it. Why?

Because many Christians fail to study the Word of God, they cannot *know* God's will and revealed truth. It is sad that so many apostate pastors and other Christians are led by the "spirit of the age" to believe the church is outdated, irrelevant and utterly confused. Meanwhile, the true [Spiritual] church refuses to accept, or adjust to their beliefs, values and anti-Christian worldview of human progress.

Secular humanists and other progressives believe that human progress in the world has affected a difference in God's plan, so they teach that the

Church must make the necessary *adjustments* [to keep up?] by rethinking God, Christ, the Holy Spirit and all Christian doctrine to keep in step with society's humanistic thoughts.

They no longer make proper adjustments because:

- They no longer read and accept the Bible as final authority in all of life.
- They know the truth and still accept the lie that the Bible is outdated.
- They are an anti-moral force, conformed or shaped by the spirit of the age.

I'm sure you readily see this faction of humanity doesn't want God over them. In fact, they demand that they are gods unto themselves. Satan is behind this devious deception to win the *hearts* of the people to follow him. Remember, what he cannot destroy, he contaminates! Folks it's not about humanity, or places or things – it's about the One Holy, *Immutable* God, Creator of all humankind, whom we are to worship, follow, obey and glorify!

For fifteen hundred years God localized Himself among His people in the tabernacle and the temple where He dwelt, a fiery manifestation, "Shekinah Glory" in the Holy of Holies. He was not teaching Israel the holiness of people, places and things, but He was teaching them the holiness of God.

When Christ died on the cross, the veil in the temple ripped open from top to bottom. Showing that the tabernacle was one holy place not two. Thus, the Holy of Holies was opened to everyone who would enter by faith alone. This principle is still true today and totally unscathed by the philosophical thoughts and actions of human beings [prayerfully study in unison (Romans 8, 9, 10).

But Christ came as High Priest of the good things to come, with the greater and more perfect tabernacle not made with hands, that is, not of this creation. Not with the blood of goats and calves, but with His own blood He entered the Most Holy Place once for all, having obtained eternal redemption. For if the blood of bulls and goats and the ashes of a heifer, sprinkling the unclean, sanctifies for the purifying of the flesh, how much more shall the blood of Christ, who through the eternal Spirit offered Himself without spot to God, cleanse your conscience from dead works to serve the living God?

Christ's Words remembered

The words that Christ spoke to the woman at the well were remembered,

"The hour cometh, when ye shall neither in the mountain, nor in Jerusalem, [place is no longer designated] *worship the Father .... But the hour comes, and now is when the true worshippers shall worship the Father inspirit and in truth for the Father seeks such to worship Him. God is a Spirit: and they that worship him must worship Him in spirit and in truth"* (John 4:21, 23-2). KJV)

God promises in His Word that, worship in spirit and truth is the worship He is seeking. Therefore, our worship must match the very nature of God. Also, we must thoroughly understand what spirit is – to aid us in being the worshippers God is seeking. It is important for us to understand that the human spirit is the primary concern in true worship because God Himself is Spirit and true worshippers must worship "in spirit and in truth." This worship comes from those who are:

- Born from above, believers destined by their new divine nature
- Thoroughly committed to Christ
- Inwardly purified by the blood of Jesus
- Separated from the world [systems]
- Not conformed or shaped by the world
- Does all to the glory of God

Spirit, soul, and body

Unfortunately, the human spirit has been relatively *overlooked* even in Christian theology. To the unsaved person the soul comprising the mind, will, emotions, attitudes, worldviews, personality, conflicts and all the rest that they are – is primarily their focus. The human spirit in the unsaved is dead [spiritually] because of inherited sin from Adam. Therefore, the mind is elevated in the thinking of many philosophers and theologians to a position of leadership over the other components, the soul and the body.

With the human spirit out of circulation, the soul takes charge of the whole being. This makes humans "soulish," not "spiritual" without which communication with God is nil or non-existent. In the unsaved state human beings are alienated from God. Is there any wonder why society is "feeling" oriented today?

Early in the twentieth century atheists and secular humanists took advantage of a lull in church leadership, and through assumptions from science and cultural reasoning began a mind-march influencing, manipulating, and gobbling up all aspects of society: the courts, education [K – PhD], the media, governments, local boards, religion and public opinion across America with the agenda to secularize it.

Certainly, many of us must admit that America today is no longer the nation we were born and raised in. The humanists' and atheists' successes have allowed them to promote their secular agenda and use these areas of influence as their secret weapons focused on the destruction of Christianity, all absolutes, all forms of authority and I believe even the destruction of the United States and Western Civilization.

The rejection of God

Targeted to be rejected in this satanic ploy is God, Christ, the Gospel, the Church, truth of God's Word, believers, and the things of God. The Scripture makes clear God's position. The apostle Paul says,

"Now may the God of peace Himself sanctify you completely; and may your whole spirit, soul, and body be preserved blameless at the coming of our Lord Jesus Christ" (1 Thessalonians 5:23 KJV). Emphasis mine throughout.

"For the Word of God is living and powerful and sharper than any two-edged sword, piercing even to the division of spirit and soul, and of joints and marrow, and is a discerner of the thoughts and intents of the heart" Hebrews 4:12 KJV).

Paul's comprehensive reference to the term "completely" emphasizes God's order which prioritizes first "spirit, then the soul, and the body" [the whole person from the (spirit) inside out in contrast to Satan's order of preference "body, soul, and spirit" [from the outside inward, from "the flesh"].

Body and soul

If a person does not believe that Americans prize their body over the other two components of their being, we'll let a little research reveal the billions of dollars spent annually on gyms, cosmetics, body building drugs, surgery, dieting, and exercise, just to name a few expenditures in this country on the body alone. The idea is to maintain the fifth avenue "look," as long as possible. In many instances, the body rules the whole being; while the soul starves to death; because of that – *we experience lust and desire for sin.* Inside of each of us, *a nature that drove us toward sin.* But the moment we were "born again," you are no longer being driven toward sin by some part of you that is by nature a child of the devil – the old body of sin must go! All that is happening is a part of Satan's playing tricks with your mind. He plays on the old thought patterns, mindsets and lies that we had toward sin. If not, careful we could react the same way we did before accepting Christ.

It's our *unrenewed* mind that drives us to sin. To overcome this, we must conclude that it's all in the mind – and not real! We "reckon" ourselves dead to the old man and alive to Christ, therefore, we control our reaction to this spiritual conflict in our minds. The key to the Christian life is the Spirit of God and renewing of the mind (Romans 12:2 KJV) and that happens only through the cleansing Word of God. When you were born again, your spirit changed – but your natural mind did not.

God gave you a new *divine* nature, all you need in your born-again spirit, but it manifests to the degree that you allow the indwelling Spirit and the Word to renew your mind. Stop hanging onto this wrong idea and stinking thinking that you are just a sinner saved by grace. Declare that old nature dead and gone – and you are now dead with Christ to sin. What you are dealing with now is what Romans 6:6 calls "the body of sin." Like the physical body requires a daily diet of food for survival; so, the spirit and soul require a consistent daily diet of spiritual food, the Word of God! Therefore, with a renewed mind we should not serve sin. Now we *destroy* the body of sin; systematically tearing down those wrong thoughts, and emotions with the Word of God replacing them with godly thoughts and emotions.

A living sacrifice [Temple of the Holy Ghost]

In Romans 12:1 KJV, Paul exhorts believers "by the mercies of God to present your bodies a living sacrifice, holy, and acceptable unto God, which is your reasonable service [*spiritual worship*]." Meaning that believers should use their bodies [the temple of the Holy Spirit] to serve and obey the Lord (see Romans 6:13). Now that the body is holy and sanctified for the Lord's use; and acceptable and pleasing to Him demonstrates that such a gift is the only rational reaction to all the good gifts of provision and protection God has showered upon us. Give Him Praise and glory. I have heard people express their willingness to die for Jesus; and that is courageous. However, I do not believe God necessarily wants you to die in these perilous times. He wants us to give ourselves away. He wants us to live for Jesus. He wants each of us to be *"a living sacrifice."*

He wants us to be holy and whatever we do – whatever we eat – or drink; God wants us to do it as an act of worship – for His glory (see I Corinthians 10:31 KJV).

Under the old Mosaic sacrificial system, the victims were always slain. But since Jesus' one sacrifice for sin, once and for all, has been accomplished on Calvary there is no further need for *dead* sacrifices. As I said earlier, what God wants is that we present ourselves to Him a living sacrifice, putting ourselves totally into His hands for His pleasure and glory. Therefore, Paul is seeking for spiritual sacrifices in the precious name of Jesus (also see I Peter 2:5 KJV).

This "living sacrifice" of the New Testament is in glorious contrast to the "dead" legal sacrifices of the Old Covenant:

- The death of the "Lamb of God, which takes away the sin of the world" (John 1:29 KJV) has done away with all dead sacrifices from the altar of God, thus making room for the redeemed children of God themselves as "living sacrifices" to God, who "made Him [Christ] to be sin for us" (II Corinthians 5:21 KJV).
- Every outgoing act of a Christian's heart in grateful praise and every act prompted by the love of Christ, is itself an act of worship to our God – a sacrifice to God of a sweet-smelling savor (see Hebrews 13:15, 16 KJV).

As the Leviticus sacrifices were offered without blemish to God; so were our members regarded as holy, so are believers, yielding themselves to God *"as those that are alive from the dead, and their members as instruments of righteousness unto God* (John 6:13 KJV) are in God's eyes "holy" and "acceptable unto Him." Again, when we have done those things which are acceptable to God, we should realize that what we have done is an act of service [worship].

Conformity

"Do not be conformed to this world [this present evil society, age]." Instead of allowing the world to conform, mold or fashion you by their political correctness and ungodly values; which are not the same as ours [same terms but different meanings]. The believer is commanded to "be transformed by the renewing of your mind" (Romans 12:2); which is truly essential for *spiritual worship*. "For all that is in the world:

- The lust of the flesh – the word "lust" does not necessarily mean sensual pleasures. It simply means "desires." These desires are at work in the members of the body, and they excite the flesh and create problems. Please keep in mind that the body itself is not sinful. It's the "fallen nature" that would control the body that is sinful. The flesh is human nature apart from God, just as the world is human society apart from God (see James 4:1-3 KJV).
- Friendship with the world – when the believer becomes a friend of the world, he or she becomes at enmity with God; which grieves the Spirit within, who jealously yearns for our love and faithfulness. The lack of true separation in the lives of many Christians is so close to the world, that it is difficult to tell whether they are saved or not (see v. 4 KJV).
- The pride of life – when Christians live for the flesh and the world they become proud. Pride is right up there with deception among the devil's tools. According to Luke 4:1-13, the Christian is admonished to use the Word of God to resist the devil and he will flee from you – the Spirit of God will enable us to do so; just as in the example of our Lord, Jesus Christ. Every Christian should be reminded that God cannot help one who is full of pride; who refuses to repent of sin and humble themselves. Grace is for the lowly – not the lofty (see vv. 6-7 KJV).

We must submit to God then we can effectively resist the devil. It is imperative that each Christian examine their own heart to see if any of these three enemies are working in us. Remember, neither of the three is of the Father, but all are of the world. And the world will surely pass away, "and the lusts thereof: but he that does the *will of God* abides forever" (see I John 2:15-17 KJV).

It is God's will that we submit our spirit, soul, and body unto Him. The church has not shown herself to be very faithful in demonstrating holiness [separation unto God]. A check of the local newspaper will reveal church leaders as well as members consorting with same sex unions, marriages, cohabitation and abortions.

The truth of the matter is that too many Christians are viewing Christianity as a self-improvement and guide to prosperous living. The command to holiness, and the essentials for such change is ignored today or re-defined. Therefore, many Christians as well as unbelievers confuse holiness with following a long list of legalistic do and do nots or they try to adjust their piety to doing religious duties. True holiness means loving God and others more than yourself.

We are to be holy as Christ is holy and through holy and righteous living share in God's redeeming work in this evil world

---

Transformed

In Hebrews 4:12 KJV, God gives us insight into the transforming power of the Word of God which separates our born again from above spirit from our sin-distorted soul which comprises our will, mind, and affections. Once these components are cleansed through the cross of Christ; then our spirit is joined back to the now renewed soul forming a true heart for God.[7]

Through the Word of God, we become discerning about the things we see in the secular culture without God all around us. This means developing a healthy worldview formed by the Spirit through the Word of God. Seeking the mind of Christ is seeing things in the world from God's perspective and acting accordingly. This is God's deterrent to a secularistic, narcissistic and materialistic society such as ours that:

- Exalts the "self" and "pleasure" instead of God and the things of God.
- Lives a self-directed life that distorts our view of others.
- Tends to think more highly of one's self than he or she ought to think.

True holiness that thinks more of God and others than yourself is rooted in true humility – the most elusive of all virtues. Humility means total dependence upon the Lord for everything! True spiritual growth is then inevitable! The recipe for growth to maturity happens when we commit "every thought, word or act" as worship unto God. Stated in a song the youth of the church sings:

"Read your Bible and pray every day, pray every day; and you'll grow, grow, and grow! And you'll grow, grow, grow, and you'll grow, grow, grow." Repeat

"Don't read your Bible and pray every day and you'll shrink, shrink, shrink."

"And you'll shrink, shrink, shrink, and you'll shrink, shrink, shrink." Repeat.

The rejection of the Gospel

Jesus sent out seventy of His followers two by two to the surrounding towns where He was about to go. Their mission was to tell the good news. If the people of the town reject you, go out into the streets and tell them, "Even the dust of your city we wipe from our feet as a warning against you. Nevertheless, know this, that the kingdom of God has come near you" (see Luke 10:10-11).

We live in a time when many people will not respond to you and flatly reject the gospel as not needed and antiquated. Certainly, we face this problem in the local churches where people will attend services every week, but persistently reject the invitation to eternal life. We need to follow Christ's instructions to warn and then back off with some of them; otherwise over a period they will become hardened. It is crucial that we understand, this is not a fleshly move on our part, but it must be by spiritual discernment to know when it is time to warn them and back off. Sometimes a hard warning is all it takes. I stated earlier, God's comission belongs to every believer in every place!

One of the reasons that many problems in the local churches are never solved, is that the person blames their problems on any and everything except their own separation from God! If this nation continues in sin, not only those of the flesh, but those in our local churches result in:

- waning love for Christ, one another, and lost souls.
- love abates and lawlessness abounds.
- the inability to speak the truth in love even toward their enemies, plainly indicate that our love is at a new low (Revelation 2:4).

If America along with the local churches repent and acknowledge that we have brought some of this upon ourselves with making ungodly life styles, rejection of God's truth, distortion of the gospel silent issues of the church. Then, realize the importance of spiritually reviving our local church's prayer ministry and restore Christ and the Bible back to the center – we will experience great revival (see 2 Chronicles 7:14).

Likewise, if we would prayerfully come and tell people the truth about Jesus' redemption and forgiveness – they will repent and be saved (see Romans 10:9-10).

It seems more church leaders would rather talk about their *power,* be it in attendance numbers or building sizes over repentance and Christian love. But no matter the shortcomings that is what made America strong and that is what will make this nation great in the coming days. As God's witnesses in a fallen world, we should make sure that what we preach and teach as the gospel of Christ is truly the pure gospel. The only way we can do that is by returning to what the Bible has to say about it, Paul says, *"it is the power of God unto salvation"* (Romans 1:16).

Moreover, brethren, I declare unto you the gospel which I preached unto you, which also you have received, and wherein you stand; by which also you are saved, if you keep in memory what I preached unto you, unless you have believed in vain. For I delivered unto you first of all that which I also received, how that Christ died for our sins according to the scriptures;

and that He was buried, and that He rose the third day according to the Scriptures (1 Corinthians 15:1-4 KJV).

This is the gospel of Christ in its true scriptural form, the "Good News." However, the Greeks did not believe in the resurrection of the dead (see Acts 17:32). The Corinthians did not doubt the resurrection of Christ; therefore, Paul initiated his argument for the resurrection of the human body. The resurrection of Christ is a historic fact authenticated by:

1. The message of the Gospel
2. The testimony of witnesses
3. The conversion of Paul himself

I know that you Corinthians believe in the resurrection of Christ, for if you didn't your faith would be vain (empty). In His resurrection body Christ appeared to the disciples in a room without anyone opening the door for His entrance. If He has a glorified body in heaven, we believers should also have one there. Thus, because of our union with Christ, just as He has been glorified, one day we also shall be glorified. Give Him praise and glory!

Restoring the spirit and practice of the Early Church

The culture agrees with the progressive thinkers, whose view includes a progressive plan in which the church would make necessary adjustments to accommodate secular cultural thinking. The true early apostolic model of Christianity had no place for deviations from the biblical spiritual Church life.

The desire to return to the practices of the early apostolic Church seems to be one of the main motivations of the thousands of Christians leaving the traditional and institutional churches. Many of these churches have become overloaded with the various secularly-instituted religious forms and practices, organizational technics and other excess baggage influenced by the secular culture. These false forms have displaced the simple biblical Christian holiness lifestyle. The true is only found in the intimate fellowship of sincere believers as instituted by the Spirit and the Word of God in apostolic ministry [organism]. To do so really restores the authentic New Testament norms recorded in the Book of Acts and the Letters; which certainly retores sacredness and significance to the faith.

The increasingly secular and anti-Christian world that we face daily is blurring the "truth of God's Word" among the millennial causing many to lean to their own understanding or involve themselves with many faiths and in many cases, no faith. The idea of more than one-way to God is catching on among the young people in the local churches. It seems that many of them feel that biblical morality is relative; therefore, they can cohabitate, involve themselves freely in heterosexual sexual acts as a rite of passage despite available biblical teaching on the subject [ignored or left to the secular educational system].

Church discipline and training is biblical

Many pastors and other Christian leaders owe the people in their sphere of influence and apology for leaving basic biblical teaching and training to the family [they say!]. And Church discipline is a dinosaur to many as it was put on the back-shelf decades ago. The church must exercise discipline to remain *doctrinally* pure. In my book *According to Pattern*, I discuss in detail, basic doctrinal training and church discipline (Scripturally).[8]

QUESTIONS FOR DISCUSSION AND REFLECTION: CHAPTER 1

1. Discuss steps to bring the local church into being "relevant to the needs of the people" (biblically).
2. Discuss the influence of "the theory of evolution" on today's local church, public education, academia and society.
3. Explain how your every act can be worship to God.
4. Discuss the misgivings of the sacred /secular philosophy and how it hinders the true spirituality of Christians today.
5. Relate the instructions Christ gave His disciples in Luke 10:10-11 to the witness of the local churches.

CHAPTER TWO

GRACE THROUGH FAITH

"For by grace you have been saved through faith, and that not of yourselves; it is the gift of God, not of works, lest anyone should boast" (Ephesians 2:8-9 KJV).

There are countless sincere, well-meaning people in the local churches everywhere who feel that they must do something to help *earn* their salvation. They devote themselves to such things prayer, penance, fasting, charity, self-denial, careful observance of church ordinances, all to no avail. They never obtain true peace with God because just like His people of old Israel; they seek peace not by grace through faith but by works righteousness.

GRACE IS FREE – BUT IT IS NEVER CHEAP!
– R.T. KENDALL

They go about to establish what is right in their own eyes – and in this way, they reject the righteousness of God, which is through grace by *faith* in Jesus Christ alone.

Saved and know it

We choose to receive God's *free* grace gift by faith – when we receive Jesus Christ as our personal Savior, in Him we receive the gift of eternal life.

"Not by works of righteousness which we have done, but according to His mercy He saved us, through the washing of regeneration, and renewing of the Holy Spirit" (Titus 3:5 KJV).

Nothing is plainer than that. Not by our own works of righteousness we have done – but solely on the mercy of God may we receive salvation. Two parts of God's plan of salvation had been fulfilled – Jesus had been crucified and raised from the dead. Two Old Testament prophesies of the events are (Psalm 118:22; Isaiah 52:15 KJV).

He is risen in deed!

After His resurrection, people had to change their minds to serve Him for who He really is, the Son of God. This is the message Peter preached at Pentecost, a message that resulted in three thousand people declaring Jesus as their Lord and Savior. Before He left, Jesus clearly summarized the mission of His disciples from Pentecost until He returns:

Then He said to them, *"These are the words which I spoke to you while I was still with you, that all things must be fulfilled which were written in the Law of Moses and the Prophets and the Psalms concerning Me."* And He opened their understanding, that they might comprehend the Scriptures. Then He said to them, *it is written,* **and thus it was necessary for the Christ to suffer and to rise from the dead the third day, and that <u>repentance</u> and <u>remission of sins</u> should <u>be preached in His name to all nations</u> beginning in Jerusalem** (Luke 24:44-47 KJV). Emphasis added.

This mandate for true gospel preaching is the same today:

- Calling people to (repentance) turn from their own selfish ways to Christ, the One who had died for them.
- God's gracious offer of (forgiveness) to all who would believe in His name. Forgiveness and blessing are received solely through faith in Christ's finished work (see Acts 2:30-39).
- Jesus pointed out that the disciples were called to testify (witness) to His work (see Acts 1:8 KJV).
- The message of Christ's salvation offer is made to anyone who will receive it (see Acts 10-15 KJV).

The Promise

Behold I send the Promise of My Father upon you; but tarry in the city of Jerusalem until you are endued with power from on high" (Luke 24:49 KJV).

The Promise of My Father is about the:

- Baptism of the Holy Spirit at Pentecost (see Acts 2 KJV).
- This outpouring was promised in Joel 2:28; also (see Acts 2:14-18 KJV).
- Peter called this coming of the Spirit "the beginning" (see Acts 11:15 KJV).

The real fulfillment of God's promise of salvation would begin here in these people united by the Holy Spirit to establish the church. However, they were helpless until they were endued with power from on high; and it remains so to this day!

In the natural order of life, if a person is alive, his or her human spirit dwells within them. Every *act* of the person's body is an expression of his or her spirit. The actual existence and character of the spirit within though invisible, are clearly revealed through the behavior and the actions of the believer's heart.

So, it is with the Spirit of faith (see 2 Corinthians 4:13) within the true Christian – active and alive. Being born again and endued with power from on high – the Spirit brings down the very life of God Himself, in Christ, to dwell within the heart of the believer. If the outward acts of faith are not manifested in the person's life; then his or her works do not correspond to the Christian faith professed indicating there is no real living faith within.

The life of worship

The life of worship within the Christian takes control of his or her whole nature – thoughts, desires, words and actions. The Christian begins to think, speak and act in a new way. He or she now does things they neither could nor would have done before the life of God came in through faith and took control of them.

Now the person has sanctified the Lord in their heart – they no longer commit common sinful acts. All acts done afterward are good and acceptable worship to God through our Lord and Savior, Jesus Christ.

And they lived happily ever after?

We are a work in progress. As God's workmanship, each of us is re-created by the Father [in regeneration], in Christ, and is being conformed to the image of His Son through the powerful ministry skills of the Holy Spirit.

This transformation does not take place through one-size-fits-all formulas but occurs through belonging to a Christian community (church) a unity of believers, who immerses us into the doctrine, doxology, and discipleship of *"teaching them to observe [obey] all that I have commanded you"*(Matthew 28:20a KJV); *"the faith that was once delivered to the saints"* (Jude 3 KJV).

We are increasingly becoming a society that is losing its inherited wisdom and craftsmanship. There is no wonder then, why the church is losing its inherited wisdom and habits of discipleship. We hear many clichés offered as a quick fix:

- One person offers that we just need to get with the program.
- Another offers that we just need to get the doctrine right.

Neither answer gets to the point that growing up into Christ cannot be reduced to intellectualism. There is no doctrinal proposition or spiritual program that can conform us to the image of Christ. The gospel must transform us over a lifetime of faith and commitment to the Lord.

New converts to "the faith" need transformation through the cleansing Word of God and time to mature – they need pastors. They need to belong to a community of Bible-believing disciples – older believers, fellow saints from various walks of life and ethnic backgrounds, who know what it means to love and trust in Christ and serve their neighbors in love.

The Bible through the Holy Spirit guides us, but there are no quick fix or how-to programs in it. God's story that gives rise to the doctrines, the ordinances of baptism and the Lord's Supper, our holy habits of faith, praise and worship, prayer and teaching, and giving of our resources is our final authority.

It takes a lot of work. Although we are not working for our salvation, we are working out our salvation as God works it in us, *"both to will and to work for His good pleasure"* (Philippians 2:13 KJV).

Even private spiritual disciples will not be of benefit in shaping our Christian discipleship without the ordinary means of grace in the church and the distinct type of holy living that arises out of it. Even at the end of our days, we will not be a finished work of Christ. Notice how Paul sums it up:

Pressing Toward the Mark

"Not that I have already attained, or am already perfected; but I press on, that I may lay hold of that for which Christ Jesus has also laid hold of me. Brethren, I do not count myself to have apprehended; but one thing I do, forgetting those things which are behind and reaching forward to those things which are ahead, I press toward the goal for the prize of the upward call of God in Christ Jesus. Therefore, let us, as many as are mature, have this mind; and if in anything you think otherwise, God will reveal even this to you. Nevertheless, to the degree that we have already attained, let us walk by the same rule, let us be of the same mind" (Philippians 3:12-16 KJV).

Paul could in no way obliterate the past from his memory, [he wanted to forget his self-righteous past], but he refused to let his past obstruct his progress toward his goal. Paul used the present tense for *"forgetting."* Paul was indicating it is an ongoing process.

Self-righteousness

Ironically, the Pharisees did not see themselves as Paul did. They did not see themselves as God's enemy, but as His chosen spiritual police force. They lived a non-spiritual natural life, pretending they had no need for forgiveness. Is there any wonder Jesus called them "snakes" and "vipers?" The Pharisees had one giant fallacy about them. They failed to realize that *redemption* comes before *righteousness*. Those who thinks they can reverse that order; probably think they can somehow redeem themselves. Jesus said,

"Woe to you, teachers of the law and Pharisees, you hypocrites! ... On the outside you appear to people as righteous but, on the inside, you are full of hypocrisy and wickedness" (Matthew 23:27-28 KJV).

Anybody who thinks they can work up righteousness by sweat does not understand true Christianity at all. Paul said, *"For if righteousness could be gained through the law, Christ died for nothing"* (Galatians 2:26 KJV).

When Christ died on the cross, He put an end to the Old Testament law: *"Christ is the end of the law so that there may be righteousness for everyone who believes"* (Romans 10:4 KJV). "End" in the context, it means "fulfillment." Because Jesus fulfilled the law perfectly, we are freed from its condemnation and guilt. However, we should still follow its moral and ethical precepts out of love for Christ. Paul wrote in his letter to the Galatians, we are now under the Law of Christ, not the Law of Moses (Galatians 6:2 KJV).

As Christ-followers, we obey because we are grateful! Jesus gave us a two-part directive:

"Love the Lord your God with all your heart and with all your soul and with all your mind .... And love your neighbor as yourself" (Matthew 22:37-39 KJV).

There is an old poison going around today with new wrapping. And that is none other than the Hyper-grace teaching which passes on the notion that believers "do not need to confess their sins" to God (God forbid!). This teaching has found its way into many churches around the world – and it is dividing families and the people of God as it goes. Paul admonished the Galatians,

"I marvel that you are turning away so soon from Him who called you in the Grace of Christ, to a different gospel, which is not another; but there are some who trouble you and want to pervert the gospel of Christ" (Galatians 1:6-7 KJV).

Despite all the allies had done and said to keep them, the Russians departed after World War II. Their departure has been a thorn in the side of the Western Nations' to this day. This passage of Scripture indicates that the Galatian believers were voluntarily deserting *grace* to return to *legalism* taught by false teachers. Paul further countered in Galatians 5:4 KJV:*"You have become estranged from Christ, you who attempt to be justified by law; you have fallen from grace."*

The word "estranged" has become a household word these days meaning "to be separated" or "to be severed" as we see among marriages and local churches today. Paul's charge is very severe, in his clear meaning that: any attempt to be justified by the law is to reject salvation by grace alone through faith alone and have "fallen from grace." The Apostle John says, their desertion of Christ and the gospel only proves that their faith was never genuine (study also: 1 John 2:9; Luke 8:13-14; Hebrews 6:4-6 KJV).

QUESTIONS FOR DISCUSSION AND REFLECTION:
CHAPTER 2

1. Contrast those receiving salvation through faith and those seeking salvation by works.
2. Discuss how we receive eternal life.
3. Discuss four facts concerning the way God's salvation works in the Christian's life.
4. From our study in this chapter, what condition in the individual proves there is no living faith within him or her?
5. The life of worship within the Christian takes control of his or her whole nature – thoughts, desires, words and actions. Discuss how this takes place:

CHAPTER THREE

THE RIGHTEOUSNESS OF GOD

"Even the righteousness of God which through faith in Jesus Christ to all and on all who believe: for there is no difference:for have sinned and fall short of the glory of God" (Romans 3:22, 23 KJV).

"The righteousness of God" is God's own righteousness; it is "Christ in you – the hope of glory" (Colossians 1:27 KJV). And if Jesus is not in you, you are not righteous in God's sight. God's righteousness comes only through Christ – it is*"by the faith of Jesus Christ unto all and upon all them that believe."* The Jew and the Gentile, the wicked and the moral – all must believe, there is no difference.

The righteousness and the holiness that Almighty God *requires,* the Son of God *became* – even in the flesh. The Holy Spirit tells us the truth concerning why Jesus came into the world and what He accomplished while here:

- "To give His life a ransom for many" (Matthew 20:28 KJV).
- "We walk in the Spirit" (Galatians 5:16 KJV).
- "We are taught by the Spirit" (I John 2:20, 27 KJV)

At the very beginning of this Epistle, Paul declared that the Gospel is,

"The power of God unto salvation to everyone that believeth to the Jew first, and also to the Greek." He then goes on to say,

"For therein is the righteousness of God revealed from faith to faith: as it is written, 'The just shall live by faith" (Romans 1: 17 KJV).

Memorize these points:

- God's righteousness is not by works, but by faith in the finished work of the Lord Jesus Christ (II Corinthians 5:21 KJV).
- All people need to be saved because "all have sinned and come short of the *glory of God"* (Romans 6:23 KJV).
- All we like sheep have gone astray; we have turned everyone to his own way; and the Lord hath laid on Him the iniquity of us all (Isaiah 53:6 KJV).
- The "glory of God" in these passages probably means Jesus Christ Himself as *God's standard* – **"the brightness of His glory"** (Hebrews 1:3 KJV). Certainly, all have come short of the glory of God in that sense.
- All people belong to God by creation, the devil never created a man, nor could he ever create a man – but only those who are saved belong to God by *redemption.*
- Jesus [*whom God hath set forth to be a propitiation*][9] bought back everything Adam sold to the devil in the Garden of Eden (see Romans 3:24-26 KJV).

The world in the New Testament meaning is, simply unregenerate human nature wherever it is found, whether in a bar or in a church.
– A. W. Tozer

As I stated in the last chapter, many who could do non-ordained Christian public service or witnessing for the Lord throughout the marketplace are ineffective toward glorying in the Lord. Because they are caught up with the old places and things (sacred) or (secular) view of the world. The average Christian thinks of his or her daily employment as secular, rather than performing their vocation as an act of worship acceptable unto God by Jesus Christ.

Often the thinking is, God can't be in this place! The story is told of an evangelist during a revival asking the members to bring and unsaved person to the meeting tomorrow night. One lady came to the evangelist after service emotionally upset exclaiming, "I don't know any unsaved people!" If she like so many other Christians were pressed for the reason, they don't know any unsaved people; would all answer "Separation from the world?"

I read an article about a man driving pass a church one Sunday morning, he saw a fellow employee from his job entering the church. The next morning, he asked the man if he was a Christian and how long he had been attending church. He answered, that he has been a Christian and church worker for many years. Puzzled his friend asked him why he kept it a secret and why didn't he invite him to go with him sometime. Of course, the Christian stood there dumb-founded!

A newspaper carried the story concerning a mailperson delivering the mail just prior to Christmas Eve who decided to hide a large batch of Christmas cards rather than deliver them. Through this act the people never received the message sent to them. Like this mailperson we are guilty when we refuse to deliver the message of the gospel of Christ to this dying world. Many people are going into eternity without Christ daily, because we choose to hide the message of salvation from them by our silence.

I'm sure that Satan is pleased with this distorted thinking; since he probably gave them the thought in the first place. Certainly, such attitude is not a standard found in the New Testament. One day on the 700 Club a Los Angeles policemen who was a Christian was featured whose daily duty is among the homeless people in the skid-row section. His first statement was he didn't want the assignment, yet, once there he fell in love with the people and they fell in love with him. It shows! He sees that God has called him to that kingdom out-post.

I accepted the call of God to the gospel ministry while in the Army and was even privileged to serve a congregation as a bi-vocational pastor for five years prior to my retirement from the Army after 26 ½ years of service. That proved to be an invaluable experience. I met my first determined atheists in the military. Additionally, I was ignored and loathed by some but loved by many including my superiors. My family and I lived an openly-involved Christian life twenty-four seven. It was a beautiful life; and just as Nichodemus did Christ – many came to us by night!

We have a much more complex world today. In society, political-correctness and partisan politics pulvarise the truth of God's Word with ever-increasing numbers. It seems that truth to a certain extent is determined or challenged by the news media, public opinion, academia, politics, even government, and sadly many pulpits.

That's why secular humanists are so successful promoting their agenda – they probe the family and the local Christian Church's growing vulnerability; which is caused by voluntary spiritual and biblical ignorance among Christians. They knowingly or unknowingly assimilate the tenets of their secular agenda and endorse them throughout much of the Christian community while secular humanists happily watch.

I said in an earlier section that public poll after poll shows that most people stated the lack of Bible reading is the cause of this country's ills. I have been confronted by some individuals in the local churches, at seminars, workshops and conferences for using the word "ignorance;" not especially from intellectuals, but mostly by people who seem to study the Bible on a lower-to-no priority and just concoct a theology based on hear say, and Bible study notes.

Many Christians today knowingly and publicly support people and that go against God's moral Law, biblical worldview, and moral principles. I'm not talking about people of other beliefs, just Christians. I often wonder if those who do so have ever considered the fact that in rejecting the Bible which is the Word of God means you are rejecting God, the Author.

Whatever Satan cannot conquer – he contaminates!

For those who hear the gospel, believe it, repent and receive it in their hearts – in obedience to the truth of God's Word are saved. The Spirit of Truth will lead and guide believers into all truth and understanding. Read your Bible and let the Spirit speak truth into your heart.

Let the Spirit and the Word deliver you from any wrong thinking to the knowledge of the truth. The faithful Spirit-filled child of God remains God's best deterrent against evil on this planet. Christ is our "All in All!"

For His glory

Now that we see the truth, we must determinedly practice living all aspects of our life for the glory of God by:

- Growing in the knowledge of our Lord and Savior, Jesus Christ.
- Meditating upon His Word day and night.
- Talking things over with the Lord in prayer.
- Being ever mindful of His glory as we move among people.
- Enjoy the sense that we all belong to God; therefore, there is no point where the sacred ends and secular begins for us.

Old habits die hard. It will be wise that we ask the Spirit to help us in deliverance from the old places and things theology. Satan will not be happy and will do all he can to derail you. I'm reminded of Martin's old hymn of the church:

"God Will Take Care of You"

"Be not dismayed what-ever be-tide – God will take care of you."

Beneath His wings of love abide – God will take care of you.

God will take care of you, thro' every day, o'er all the way;

He will take care of you – God will take care of you."

I cannot over emphasize, we must offer all our acts to God in faith and believe He will accept them. Then stand fast to your position insisting that every act of every day and night is unto the Lord. Let us believe

God is in all our deeds no matter how simple they may seem – and we mean every act including our careers and vocations are for His glory! The Christian never needs to think of his or her world as being inferior to that of any other Christian:

- Every person is being faithful in his or her calling for it is not what a person does that determines whether their service is accepted – but why and what manner did he or she do it?
- As we are faithful in the ever so simple service, we will hear the voice of the angel saying, *"Holy, holy, holy is the LORD of hosts: the whole earth is full of His glory"* (Isaiah 6:3 KJV).

Moved from places and things

In Acts 2:40-47, we see an example of this type of living out the ministry of every act as worship to God for His glory. The apostles prayed, devoted their time to preaching, teaching, and modeling a life devoted to Christ.

The congregation met at the temple for large-group worship and teaching, and in homes where they broke bread together. They lived in a decadent culture with a corrupt government, where there was tremendous injustice, unspeakable immorality, and a god on every corner for pagan worship.

These faithful disciples were viewed as a radical cult accused of incest because of their [agape] love relationships; and they were considered atheists because they would not worship Caesar or his gods.

Yet God empowered this little countercultural group as they came together in "one another unity" and walked and talked together following in the manner of their example, Jesus Christ. They were not politically inclined, nor did they have any clout with the politicians, but they surrendered their all to Christ and met the deepest needs in their community. They did not complain, nor did they gossip or judge. They fed the poor, lived their lives together, and loved one another. *They changed the world!*

I stated in an earlier section, there is a role for *individual* Christians in politics and market place leadership [remember all belongs to God].

Without Christian influence in the various elements of government and business, how can these people possibly be moved to restrain evil? Transformation of the heart must precede lasting transformation in the culture. How can this be accomplished? The founders of Chick-fill-la and Hobby-Lobby are model Christian examples.

For me preaching and teaching the truth of God's Word is not just akin to worship; it is the *experience* of worship! Worship falls under the same theological meaning as service. When we speak of a service of worship or of a worship service, we are saying the same thing. The two words in the Greek mean the same thing. To worship God means to serve Him. There are two ways to do it:

1. One way is to do things for Him that he needs to have done – carry the gospel for Him, stand on His side, feed His sheep, etc.
2. The other way is to do things for Him that you need to do – sing for Him, give things up for Him, talk to Him about what's on your mind and in your heart, and rejoice in Him. Open your mouth and let Him speak through you.

"You shall worship the Lord your God, Him only you shall serve" (Luke 4:8 KJV).

To worship God is to serve Him exclusively; *every act of service* given to a neighbor, or in the market place [occupation] is on a deeper level, service to our God. "It is to carry His message for Him in life and manner." This manner of living out God's truth daily through concrete practices is worship.

I can not emphasize it too much, every act of caring, support, healing, giving the truth of God's Word to a neighbor, and including our honorable daily occupation [work] is a form of service and therefore an act of worship. So, when we:

Witness – I encourage the Bread of Life Bible Institute students to begin where you are [your area of influence] with your family members especially your spouse, children, grandchildren and great-grands, friends, forget not that person working next to you, the neighbor down the street, cashier at the local market – of course we will use our testimony, the Word of God, but do not forget to live out these truths in front of them, a righteous person has influence even with strangers through a life of service [worship].

Begin a Ministry – for example: feed the poor, one-on-one Bible study in Rest homes, and light home repairs, free lawn service, and visitation to the elderly [shopping for them, taking them to appointments]. One lady purchased children's jackets year-around at sales; then she would spend each winter checking school bus stops; if she spotted a child without a jacket, out of the car she jumped, opened the trunk sized up the child – and blessed him or her with a new winter jacket. Many recovered alcoholics and former drug addicts want to participate in ministry, but in many churches, they are rebuffed by the so-called clean people. However, God has not forgotten them, today many churches and small groups are adding recovery ministry to their missions.

Write a Book – for example: I am presently writing to publish my eighteenth book; since I left the pastor. At one point I've of mywondered why most minister friends are half my age; then the Spirit let me know they are receiving from me as I pour out godly wisdom and knowledge of the truth of God's Word and advice on many areas of ministry and life after more than forty years of victories and defeats in pastoral and teaching ministry.

Anointed living – at 81 and my wife 77 years old, we still have the anointing and desire to contribute to the kingdom of God. Being old Spirit-filled wineskins among many – We train, mentor and encourage others as we help to turn the pulpit over to the next generation, whose foundation must be the same one that was passed on to us [the gospel of Jesus Christ], certainly we want to keep the Gospel of Christ doctrinally pure and deeply grounded in revealed truth.

Sometimes Magdalene and I will be sitting talking about how nice and comfortable the chairs feel and how good it would be to just sit there at home. Then we get up and it's off to teach another class at the Bible Institute, preaching or teaching a workshop, seminar or consulting with a pastor or church somewhere.

We've been married for 58 years. My loving Proverb 31 wife spent 21 years traveling the world with me in the military. She was a stay-at-home mom until our five children were grown up and on their own. She went back to work and retired from her own career in public education after I retired from the U.S. Army.

We are both in good health, and we walked and hit the gym until COVID-19 closed them. This not only afforded us many witnessing opportunities, but a learning opportunity as we interacted with the millennia generation one on one. COVID-19 has really hindered our progress in this area.

We have annual physicals, but no regimens or doctor appointments in between. God is keeping us fit for the journey; and we are happy that He uses us so. What a blessing! He wants all of us to prosper and be in good health [for His glory]!

Plant a non-traditional Bible School or in-home Bible Study (Discipleship Ministry)

In August 1998 my wife Magdalene and I founded the Bread of Life Bible Institute, and Christian Center Church a non-traditional Bible-teaching and discipleship-making ministry, which serves churches, pastors, ministry leaders, and students worldwide. Our passion is to disciple and equip for kingdom service "everyday Christians" to actually "live a righteous and transformed Christian life" by raising the bar to reach maturity and be authentic and useful disciples of Jesus Christ – restoring God's truth and purpose in the local churches.

God has given us a unique ability to communicate biblical truth; enabling and challenging people to grow to spiritual maturity, as they live out their own faith and make disciples. All true Christians are New Testament ministers of reconciliation charged to obey the Great Commandment to make disciples. All should fully understand that the witnessing process is continuous on and on until Jesus Christ returns (see Matthew 28:19-20). God has given the "seed" power within [His Word] to reproduce itself all it needs is to be planted in good ground and cared for. The gospel "seed" in us, earthen vessels, which we plant in good ground expecting it to reproduce itself in other good ground, and so on. I read about a bowl of seed corn found in one of the pyramids in Egypt; after some 3000 years the pyramid was opened. The seeds were removed and planted in the ground.

The power to reproduce was still in the seeds after 3000 years and they produced a harvest of corn. If we plant the authentic gospel seed into good ground, the revealed truth, instead of our opinions, and stop regurgitating what others have said – again, the gospel "seeds" planted will produce a harvest! Carefully study and follow the Lord's multiplication [seed] plan in 2 Timothy 2:2 KJV.

Service as the way of Jesus

Service is a continuing subject in the teachings of Jesus. It was a

virtue[10] of importance to Him and He practiced it [virtue is no longer found in the societal dictionary]. If Jesus was a man who lived to serve others, then certainly the church is only the church [His body] as it exists for others in the practice of agape love. Proper practice of agape reminds me of an old railroad sign at an unguarded crossing in my childhood hometown which read: Stop, Look, and Listen:

"Stop" – we must be alert and ready to stop for God's interruptions and the service of forbearance.

"Look" – be observant of your surroundings to help the weak, the sick, and the righteous must help the fallen.

"Listen" – listening to others is an extension of the work of God, the great Listener.

Following Jesus is joining Him in the service of humanity. Throughout His teachings are the recurrent themes of the necessity and the dignity of service [acts of worship]. In his book: *"Dissident Discipleship,"* David Augsburger lists many such Scriptural themes Jesus used that we all should adhere to:

- There are truly great servants (Mark 10:44; Luke 22:26-26 KJV).
- To lead is to serve (Mark 10:44; Matthew 6:24 KJV).

- It is in caring for the other that we find our true calling (Mark 10:45; Luke 22:27 KJV).
- It is in serving that we become rich (Luke 16:13; Matthew 6:24 KJV).
- It is in giving that we receive, in losing our life that we find it (John 12:24-26 KJV).
- To serve a child is to serve God (Mark 9:36-37 KJV).
- Service nourishes humility; dominance feeds arrogance (Matthew 23:11; Luke 22:24-27; Matthew 20:25-28 KJV).
- Friendship is availability and openness to mutual service (John 15:13-17 KJV).[11]

Follow the Leader

In Jesus' last appearance to His followers after His resurrection; He empowered this diverse group of ordinary people including fishermen, tax collectors and some 120 others to do supernatural ministry by His Spirit. Then, Jesus laid out His kingdom plan for the mission to reach the nations by involving *each* of His followers until He returns. Jesus said,

"All authority has been given unto Me in heaven and on earth. Go therefore and make disciples of all the nations, baptizing them in the name of the Father, and of the Son, and of the Holy Spirit, teaching them to observe all things that I have commanded you; and lo, I am with you always even to the end of the age" (Matthew 28:18-20).

Jesus intended them to equip others for the mission, just like He had taught and modeled before them. Some how much of the American Church missed or just chose to ignore these commands. His intent was for each follower to participate in the corporate body ministry of reconciliation by leading others to Christ, baptizing, them, and [making disciples] by teaching them to observe all the things Jesus commanded.

This commission from our Lord is given to the churches [every born-again Christian]. People are less likely today to be taught "all" unless the church is obedient and do the entire commission. Witness – evangelism is an individual task incorporated into God's plan and purpose for the local Church.

Paul told his young son in the faith, Timothy, "You've heard me teach things that have been *confirmed* by many reliable witnesses. Now teach these truths to other trustworthy people who will be *good ground* and able to pass them on to others" (see 2 Timothy 2:2 KJV). Paul (1st generation) invested in Timothy (2nd generation) and then charged him to teach and equip other trustworthy people (a 3rd generation), and to help them pass it on to others also (a 4th generation). The idea is for you to invest in many people by:

- Spiritually equipping them to know and follow Jesus Christ.
- Coaching them to start small groups of their own – and repeat the process over and over – all in the context of the apostolic Church [spiritual organism rather than organization].

LO, I am with you

You "can go" and lead people to faith in Jesus Christ, and help them to identify with the Father, Son, and Holy Spirit through baptism, fellowship and spiritual formation [sanctification]. Remember all authority was given to Jesus, and He's always with you through the indwelling Holy Spirit. He commissioned you and me to make disciples.

- Every child of God has His promise that He will be with them always, by His Spirit.
- "You will receive power when the Holy Spirit comes on you; and you will be My witnesses in Jerusalem, and in all Judea, and Samaria, and to the ends of the earth" (Acts 1:8 KJV).
- God has been doing supernatural things through ordinary people for 2000 years because His Spirit is in them and has empowered them.
- The authority has been given to Him, and He is in us. It's not up to you. It's up to Him.
- It's not by your power. It's by His power. It's not by your abilities, but His abilities through you (see Romans 5:9-10 KJV).
- How wonderful it will be when Christ introduces you to those who are in heaven because of your spiritual, and influential life of witness though you never met them in person on the earth.

Jesus expects to do the same through you, you, and you! The question is, whether you believe Him and trust in Him to do in His power what you will never be able to do in your own power. Jesus invites you into His kingdom work; now just think about it you'll be gathering fruit that is eternal. If your knees are a little weak right now, give God some praise! You are where God wants you. Now realize that He wants you to fully depend on Him. The Lord told Paul,

"My grace is sufficient for you, for My strength is made perfect in weakness" (2 Corinthians 12:9 KJV).

Paul went on to say, *"When I am weak, then I am strong"* (v. 10). He not only boasted about his weakness (v. 9), he said I take pleasure in my weaknesses. In Paul's weaknesses, Christ's power was made more apparent to others. It would bring praises and glory to the only One who deserved it.

Abide in Me

Apart from Christ a believer can do nothing. Jesus said, *"I am the vine, you are the branches. He who abides in Me, and I in him, bears much fruit; for without Me you can do nothing. If anyone does not abide in Me, he is cast out as a branch ......"* (John 15:5, 6 KJV).

A branch does not have a stressful life bearing fruit, it simply remains connected to the vine and fruit is produced naturally. Jesus has all authority. He is always with us by His Spirit. As we simply learn to listen to those quit promptings in our spirit to do His will, participate in His kingdom work, and we will bear much fruit.

These truths seem to be hidden today. Christ will produce spiritual life in us and impact the world through us. Yet, there are many people – yes, truly born-again Christians who live in uncertainty and *unbelief.* They do not enjoy their spiritual birthright because they have broken fellowship with our Lord and Savior, Jesus Christ.

If they would only turn their eyes from themselves to the precious blood of Jesus, they would get rid of their unbelief and become happy Christians. Many people are hindered because they think having the faith in God will automatically produce victory in their lives. If not careful your unbelief will counterbalance your faith and short, it out – unbelief must go:

Your problem is not a lack of faith – but rather too much unbelief!

Note for example in Matthew 17:14-17 KJV, how Jesus answered the question of unbelief with His disciples. And when they had come to the multitude, a man came to Him, kneeling to Him and saying,

"Lord, have mercy on my son, for he is an epileptic and suffers severely; for he often falls in the fire and often into the water. So, I

brought him to your disciples, but they could not cure him." Then Jesus answered and said, *"O faithless and perverse generation, how long shall I be with you? How long shall I bear with you? Bring him here to Me. And Jesus rebuked the demon, and it came out of him …"*

When the disciples asked Jesus why they could not cast out the demon? Jesus said, *"Because of your unbelief"* (v. 20). Needless, to say, Jesus was displeased. This is not the way the story should end. This was an important question, because Jesus had already given them power over unclean spirits, to cast them out, and heal all manner of sickness and disease (see Matthew 10:1 KJV). And the disciples had already done so (see Mark 6:13). What was the problem? For some reason many people believe they can not have faith and unbelief at the same time. They believe that faith and unbelief are mutually exclusive, but that is not the way it is. Faith and unbelief are opposing forces:

- Unbelief counteracts your faith; so instead of trying to get more faith, you need to deal with the unbelief that is counterbalancing your faith – this is the reason for the disciples' frustrations when they could not cast the demon out of the boy (Matthew 17:19 KJV).
- True faith [without unbelief] according to Christ always involves *surrender* to the will of God. He was teaching that both the source and the object of all genuine faith – even the weak mustard-seed variety is God! (v.20); and *"with God nothing will be impossible"* (Luke 1:37 KJV). Here Christ has added the qualifying thought that is explicitly,

"If we ask anything according to His will, He hears us, whatever we ask, we know that we have the petitions that we have asked of Him" (1 John 5:14 KJV).

This phrase provides a key to answered prayer. Christians can know with absolute confidence that God *hears* and *answers* prayer:

- When the believer approaches the throne of grace (Hebrew 4:16 KJV).
- When we pray in obedience, according to His will and not our own desires or what we insist He do for us – then your faith can work, and you have the victory (John 14:13-14 KJV).
- God always hears the prayers of His children, but not always in the manner they were presented (Psalm 34:15-17 KJV).

The Church has failed to portray the Lord as the One with the answers to all the problems of life – due to unbelief. When genuine Christians know God's Word [His will] and obediently practice those things that are pleasing to Him; they will supremely seek His desires over their own (Matthew 26:39-42 KJV). Bracket is mine.

The believer who abides faithfully in Jesus Christ:

- feeding upon His Word,
- assimilating it through study, prayer and meditation
- in humble submission to the guidance of the Holy Spirit
- as the truth of God's Word is revealed,
- will find peace, satisfaction, happiness, and victory.

We are promised in Isaiah 26:3 that, "He will keep you in perfect peace, whose mind is stayed on Him: because he *trusts* in Him."

Always for the Glory of God

In all that we've covered in this chapter, the final and most important aspect of the church's purpose is the glory of God. Whether pursuing all the services and ministries listed above, this one purpose prevails. The church is *the unique instrument,* God has ordained for bringing Him such glory. According to the Bible, God's intent was:

- Through the church, the manifold wisdom of God should be made known to the *rulers* and *authorities* in the heavenly realms, according to His eternal purpose – accomplished in Christ Jesus (see Ephesians 3:10-11 KJV).

- The local church must be ever mindful that our express purpose is the spreading of God's glory throughout His creation.

These responsibilities lie not just with individual Christians or the faithful few, but with the whole congregation. It seems the world beats us at pooling resources. Together local churches can network wisdom, experiences, financial support to certain goals, prayers, and callings and direct such efforts to the common purpose of making God's glory great among all nations. The story is told of a little 5-year-old boy, who saw the need of another child on the TV; it so moved him that he put his toys in his wagon and up and down the block he went selling them to support that need. He raised a total of five dollars.

However, his effort and generosity were captured by someone who was so moved they called in the local TV news to capture it. His 5 dollars grew into thousands of dollars needed to meet the need as hundreds across the world contributed. Many local churches consider themselves too small to contribute to God's missions, that is a little selfish as we look around at the many efforts put forth like the little 5-year-old. Witnessing the glory of God proclaimed around the world in the hearts of all His people should be an end and purpose of every local Bible-believing church, to the glory of God.

QUESTIONS FOR DISCUSSION & REFLECTION: CHAPTER 3

1. Discuss reasons why some Christians consider their place of employment as secular. How should they view it?
2. Discuss the secular humanists' agenda for America.
3. We must offer all our acts to God in [] and [], He will accept them.
4. Ponder this: Read your Bible and let the Spirit of truth into your heart. Let the Spirit and the Word deliver you from the sacred and secular dilemma.
5. Transformation of the heart must precede lasting transformation in the culture.

CHAPTER FOUR

LIVING A SANCTIFIED LIFE

"We know that the law is spiritual, but I am carnal, sold under sin. For what I am doing I do not understand. For what I will to do, that I do not practice; but what I hate, that I do. If then, I do what I will not to do, I agree with the law that it is good. But now it is no longer I who do it, but sin dwells in me. For I know that in me [that is in my flesh] *nothing good dwells; for to will is present with me but has to perform what is good I do not find"* (Romans 7:14-18). Emphasis added.

When we were born again, we received God's life; which is the very beginning of the Christian walk. Only those who have believed on the death, burial and resurrection of our Lord and Savior, Jesus Christ and received eternal life are presumed to have died with Him. For those born again, there is great potentiality for spiritual growth to maturity [discipleship] through sanctification [cleansed through the Word].

Making members is not making disciples!

It is important that new born again Christians know that they must be spiritually matured and not just placed on a membership roll. The Holy Spirit will lead and guide the Christian through this phase of life. We are to give Him free reign, surrender and be obedient to His instructions. The Holy Spirit through the Word of God *can* bring the person into complete maturity and victory through sanctification.

Two kinds of Christians in the local church

In 1 Corinthians 3:1 the Apostle Paul divides all Christians into two categories – spiritual and carnal:

1. A spiritual Christian is one in whom the truth of God's Word and the Holy Spirit dwells within his or her heart and controls their entire being. Further, he or she has a renewed mind and willingly take up their cross daily – for the glory of God (see Galatians 5:16-18).
2. A carnal Christian is one who has been born again and has God's life, but instead of overcoming his or her *flesh* – that person is overcome by his or her flesh; mainly through their old nature inherited from Adam (see Galatians 6-10).

We know that the unregenerate or natural person's spirit is dead, and they are dominated by their body and soul through their five senses.

Spiritual Christians

Only when the Christian is spiritually-minded and growing in grace and the knowledge of our Lord and Savior, Jesus Christ, and *consistently* guided by the Spirit and the Word of God can salvation be wholly completed in them. God has provided full salvation in Calvary for the regeneration of sinners and complete victory over their old life.

Carnal Christians

A carnal Christian then is one whose spirit has been quickened to life, but he or she continues to be carnal-minded and follows their body and soul into sin. If a person remains in a carnal condition long after experiencing the new birth, he or she hinders God's salvation from realizing its full maturity and manifestation [salt and light] to the dark world. This is the typical born-again Christian in a church that makes mere members [the goal of too many churches], instead of making disciples [God's goal for all]. Members are not necessarily disciples (Matthew 18:19-20 KJV).

The flesh

In Romans 7:14 KJV, Paul said, "I am flesh, meaning not just his nature or some other part of him – but his whole being. He reiterates that thought again in v. 18 by restating, "within me, that is, in my flesh." In connection with this usage of "flesh" it is imperative that we remember that in the very beginning man was created spirit, soul, and body.

The soul and body can only be connected to the spiritual realm through a person's spirit. As the seat of personality and consciousness, the soul must decide whether it is to obey the spirit and be united with God and His will or yield to the body and all the temptations of the material world. In the fall of man, the soul resisted the spirit's authority and *became enslaved to the body and its passions* [flesh].

The "flesh" has four closely related meanings or designations:

1. All that an unregenerate person is.
2. The soft part of the human body; which also consist of bones and blood.
3. It broadly means the human body whether living or dead. In Romans 7, Paul related "sin of the flesh" to the human body. In v. 23, "I see in my members another law at war with the law of my mind and making me captive to the law of sin which dwells in my members." The Apostle continues in Romans 8 wherein he explains that if we are to overcome the flesh we must *"put to death the deeds of the body"* through the Spirit and the Word [sanctification] (v. 13). Emphasis added.

Hence the New Testament uses the Greek word *sarx*[12] to indicate not only *psychical flesh* but also *physical flesh*.

4. As applied to the totality of humanity and without exception, the Bible views all humanity as flesh. Every individual person is controlled by that composite of old sin nature called the flesh, [the seat of sin in humans] following both the sins of the body and the self of his or her soul. *Sarx* then, refers to human beings in total.

God's reaction to <u>all</u> sin

It has been said, "If the Word of God was a ring, and the Epistle of Romans its precious stone, chapter eight would be the sparkling point of the jewel." I think all believers agree that Romans 8 is one of the most precious and beloved chapters in the entire Word of God.

In Chapter 8 we find God's climax to the argument in Romans 3:21-31 KJV teaching us that righteousness is by faith in the finished work of Jesus Christ our Lord which teaches us that:

- The righteousness of God is through faith in the finished work of Christ (Chapter 3).
- This righteousness of God does not contradict Old Testament Scriptures (chapter 4).
- By the righteousness of God obtained through the finished work of the Lord Jesus Christ; we are *kept by the power of God* (Chapter 5).
- Sinful living is neither produced nor encouraged by the gospel teaching of salvation by grace through faith, but teaches that we are *dead* to sin and, *"alive unto God through Jesus Christ our Lord."* The born-again believer can trust in Jesus Christ to keep him or her, instead of depending on their own ability – which could *never* provide victory over the old nature. Christ's divine nature in us brings our victory (Chapter 6).
- The believer's sanctification by the Law is totally impossible (Chapter 7).
- We will learn that through the Holy Spirit who dwells within every believer, we are able to live a sanctified life – but only as we allow the Spirit and the Word of God working in tandem to cleanse, lead and guide our day by day "walk in the Spirit" (Chapter 8).

No condemnation

One of the most neglected doctrines in the Bible is that of the Holy Spirit and His ministries. It is a wonderful thing for the believer to discover the indwelling Holy Spirit as the Spirit of life, truth, and power. Undoubtedly it is impossible to be in gospel order as a New Testament Local Church without the Holy Spirit and His ministries.

Therefore, unless the local church is walking corporately and individually after the Spirit – they are walking after the flesh which brings condemnation. *Wuest's translation of the New Testament* reads in the original, "Therefore, now there is *not even one bit of condemnation to those who are in Christ Jesus"* (Romans 8:1).

We have been justified by faith in Jesus Christ (see Romans 5:1). Justification is the act of God whereby God Himself declares righteous one who believes in His only begotten Son, Jesus Christ:

- In Christ, we stand free from condemnation.
- There is no condemnation from the Law because Jesus fulfilled the Law.
- There is no condemnation because of our sin inherited from Adam, for Jesus Christ (the last Adam) *bought back* everything Adam lost – He did what the first Adam could not do.
- There is no condemnation from any source because we are *in Christ Jesus,* born of His Spirit, washed in His precious blood, *hid with Christ in God.* For His glory!
- This is not a condition whereby one may be saved – but a fact concerning one who has truly been born from above. Please note, Paul does not base this claim of no condemnation to the believer upon his or her conduct – but upon their position in Christ.

In Romans 8:2 we are taught that by the higher and more powerful *"law of the Spirit of Life"* the believer is *delivered* and *made free* from both the *"the law of sin"* and the *"law of death."*

In chapter 7 the believer is seeking to live a righteous life through the law, but at the same time the law of sin and death was warring in his mind, bringing him under subjection. Thank the Lord for chapter 8, wherein the believer through the Holy Spirit dwelling within makes him or her aware of *deliverance* through His Word abiding daily – moment by moment in their heart.

Greater Is He that is in us

By position the child of God has been liberated by Christ from the compelling power of the old evil nature and made a partaker of the divine nature, a new inner condition which when properly [nurtured in the Spirit and Truth of God's Word] produces in the Christian a desire and motive to be obedient to the Lord's commands.

I John 4:4 says, that we are overcomers because *"greater is He that is in you, than he that is in the world."* John is telling us that the Holy Spirit within is more powerful, and greater than the devil without.

Again, look at Romans 8:2 the believer is seen as yielding himself or herself to the indwelling Holy Spirit of God, who by divine power delivers the believer from the law of death. Give Him glory! By the cross of Jesus sin is condemned, for God sent Him into the world as a *sin-offering.*

All humanity has gone astray

"All have sinned and come short of the glory of God" (Romans 3:23 KJV).

"All we like sheep have gone astray; 'We have turned *everyone* to his own way; 'And the Lord, has laid on Him the iniquity of us all" (Isaiah 53:6 KJV).

All were under condemnation. Sin in the flesh – all centering in the Lamb of God on the cross – who was put to death in order that the righteousness of God (demanded by the law of God) might be *fulfilled in the believer.*

"The desires of the heart show our position spiritually."

Out of Christ

Despite what you might hear concerning people and their relationship with God. Many in the local churches today are there because numbers mean prestige. However, the Scripture says, *"So then those that are in the flesh cannot please God"* (v. 8). This is a simple statement easily understood. It is a definite declaration of God's attitude toward those who are *out of Christ.* All unbelievers are without faith, and without faith it is impossible to please Him (see Hebrews 11:6 KJV).

God deals with humankind through His Son, the Lord Jesus Christ, and only through Him. "Whosoever will, may come," but all who come to God must come God's way. Jesus said,

"I am the Way, the Truth, and the Life; no man comes to the Father except through Me" (John 14:6 KJV).

Anyone coming to God in Jesus Christ is welcome; but those who try to approach God – or try to "climb up" – some other way, are thieves and robbers (see John 10:1), and they will fail to enter the Father's house – "for there is none other name under heaven given among men, whereby we must be saved" (see Acts 4:12 KJV).

Hear the solemn oath

"Anyone who rejected Moses' law died without mercy on the testimony of two or three witnesses. Oh! How much worse punishment, do you suppose, one will be thought worthy who has trampled the Son of God underfoot, counted the blood of the covenant by which he or she was sanctified a common thing, and insulted the Spirit of grace? For we know Him who said, *"Vengeance is mine, I will repay,"* says the Lord. And again, *The Lord will judge His people."* It is a fearful thing to fall into the hands of the living God (Hebrews 10:28-31 KJV).

Paul wants us to understand clearly, that all flesh is under condemnation and the terrible wrath of Almighty God. There is no salvation, no way to approach God – except through the Lord Jesus Christ and His shed blood. Let there be no mistake, all unbelievers are treading underfoot the Son of God. By their actions:

- They are testifying that the blood of the Covenant is not clean.
- They are not willing to accept the cleansing power of the blood of Jesus, shed on the cross for the remission of sin.
- They have heard about the Son, they have heard about His death, but they are not willing to accept the Son of God as God's love-gift to them.
- They are not willing to put their trust in the shed blood of God's Son; they repudiate the blood of the everlasting covenant when they reject the finished work of Jesus Christ as the only necessity for salvation from condemnation and the eternal wrath of God.

The doctrine of the indwelling Spirit

"But you are not in the flesh but in the Spirit, if indeed the Spirit of God dwells in you. Now if anyone does not have the Spirit of Christ, he is not His. And if Christ is in you, the body is dead because of sin, but the spirit is alive because of righteousness. But if the Spirit of Him who raised Jesus from the dead dwells in you, He will also give life to your mortal bodies through His Spirit who dwells in you" (Romans 8:9-11).

Despite such powerful passages as these, research from such reputable organizations as Barna, Pew, and Gallup reflect that many local churches across America are operating without the Holy Spirit and His essential ministries; and some even go so far as denying His very presence on earth.

Despite the clear declaration of Scripture that, anyone who does such, is not one of His. In his first epistle to the Corinthians, Paul clearly stated that the body of the believer "is the temple of the Holy Spirit who is in you whom you have from God …....." And he goes on to explain that we are not our own, but we are brought with a price and therefore should glorify God in our body (I Corinthians 6:19-20 KJV).

It is sad the tremendous amount of erroneous theology concerning the Holy Spirit circulating throughout the various Christian Communities causing much deception and confusion. The Holy Spirit does not take up His abode in the believer at some time after regeneration; but the moment the unbeliever believes on the Lord Jesus Christ and is born from above by the power of the Holy Spirit, he or she is indwelt by the Holy Spirit and sealed to the day of redemption (see Ephesians 4:30; Romans 5:5, 9 KJV).

The Spirit of Christ

Anyone who claims to be a Christian and does not possess the Spirit of Christ is promoting pure error. On one occasion Jesus said, "No man can come to Me, except My Father which sent Me draw him" (John 6:44). Then Jesus taught that it is the Holy Spirit who convicts and draws people to God (see John 16:7-11). The Holy Spirit:

- Leads the believer (Romans 8:14).
- Assures the believer (Romans 8:16).
- Seals the believer (Ephesians 4:30).
- Fills the believer (Ephesians 5:18).
- Indwells the believer (Romans (8:9).
- Resides in the body of the believer (1 Corinthians 6:9-20).

I repeat: According to Romans 8:9, "If any man [or woman] has not the Spirit of Christ," he or she does not belong to God. To summarize, it is totally impossible to be saved apart from the ministry of the Holy Spirit. When Christ comes to dwell in us in the Person of the Holy Spirit, then we are dead to the "flesh" and the "law" because Christ is the end of the law for righteousness to everyone that believes (Romans 10:4). But we are alive unto God because the Spirit of God abides in us. We are partakers of the divine nature (see II Peter 1:4). Parenthesis added. In Galatians 2:20 KJV Paul told the Galatians,

"I am crucified with Christ, nevertheless I live; not I but Christ lives in me. And the life which I now live in the flesh I live by faith in the Son of God, who loved me, and gave Himself for me."

Paul was dead – but speaking; only a *spiritually-minded* person can understand that. He told the Colossians,

"You are dead, and your life is hid with Christ in God" (Colossians 3:3 KJV).

All believers are dead to the flesh – but alive unto Christ, the Covenant Head.

Heavenly places in Christ

The Scripture tells us that, *"We sit together in heavenly places in Christ Jesus"* (Ephesians 2:6). The miracle happens only through *"Christ in you"* (Colossians 1:27 KJV). In Romans 8:11 we notice a change of the name from:

- *Jesus* [the Man who died on the cross], whom God raised from the dead – to *Christ* [the New Covenant Head].
- He was raised not only as Jesus the Man, but as Jesus the Christ, who stands for all who are in Him.
- "He that raised Christ from the dead shall also quicken or make live your mortal bodies (see v. 11).
- The true children of God will never be subject to death (see II Corinthians 5:8), however the body is subject to death.
- Christians like sinners eventually die, but the spirit of the believer is absent from the body and present with the Lord (2 Corinthians 5:8 KJV).
- The spirit of the unsaved go to hades[13] to await the Great White Throne Judgment (see Revelation 20:11).
- In verse 11 the future resurrection of the believer's body is referenced. Jesus Christ, our Lord was raised from the dead [a physical resurrection].

The bodies of the dead saints will be *"quickened"* or raised from the dead, at the Rapture[14] of the Church by the Holy Spirit – *"His Spirit that dwells in you and me."* Give Him praise and glory!

Millions missing

The early breaking news around the world reported millions of people were missing. For reasons unknown to man planes were falling from the sky, ships crashing into piers pilot and captain missing, trains derailing after running miles down the track because the engineer disappeared, interstate highways clogged with wreckage due to disappearing drivers, people waking up to find their children missing, yet there is no sign of forced entry reported no where in the world. Crowded elevators stuck everywhere without operators. These scenes were repeated worldwide.

The world is in chaos. What is going on? Of course, the saints of God were not in the dark! Christ came in the air and caught His Church out of the world. We refer to this event "the blessed hope," the term Paul used in Titus 2:13: *"Looking for the blessed hope and glorious appearing of our great God and Savior, Jesus Christ."* When the Bible speaks "hope" we note it is not of something merely promised – but a fact of the future. For two thousand years when a loved one dies, he or she awaits *the resurrection of the dead* when the dead *rises first* and then those believers who are still alive will be transformed to join the Lord in the air. Paul adds, *"so shall we ever be with the Lord."*

The hundreds of references of Christ's Second Coming, it is clear that it will be in two parts:

- First the "rapture" of His Church to His Father's house (John 14:1-3 KJV) as He promised. There the saints will appear before the judgment seat of Christ (2 Corinthians 5:8-10 KJV), and the Marriage Supper of the Lamb (Revelation 19:1-10 KJV).
- Second His glorious appearing, when He will actually return to the earth gloriously and publicly in great power to set up His kingdom.

Paul exhorted the The

Paul exhorted the Thessalonians [and us] to live godly lives in light of Christ's coming judgments on the world, as the wrath of God unfolds (see Matthew 13:34-50; 24:29-44; Revelation 6-19 KJV).

QUESTIONS FOR DISCUSSION & REFLECTION: CHAPTER 4

1. Discuss the importance of the maturing process for a new-born Christian.
2. Contrast a spiritually-minded Christian with a carnally-minded Christian.
3. Discuss the four characteristics of the "flesh."
4. Contrast justification with sanctification.
5. Discuss the necessity of the infilling of the Holy Spirit.

FACE THE CHALLENGE

CHAPTER FIVE

CALLED AND EQUIPPED

"All scripture is given by inspiration of God, and is profitable for doctrine, for reproof, for correction, for instruction in righteousness: That the man of God may be perfect, thoroughly furnished unto all good works" (2 Timothy 3:16, 17 KJV).

In the text above the main point the writer emphasizes is that the Christian faith is guaranteed by its inspired Scriptures. Once written down, these become the standards *for teaching, for reproof, for correction, and for training in righteousness.* Here in the Scriptures the believer finds correct doctrine whereby he or she may refute false teaching, correct and restore with truth those who are in error. And theoretically or practically train men and women in the ways of the moral and righteous life [make disciples].

A CALL TO ARMS

The Bible, the Word of God, is unique. For example, here in just a few words is the ideal for everyone set apart for God and engaged in Christian service. That person is complete, a whole person in spirit, soul, body, and practice!

Thus, the believers can draw on the resources of their own personal experiences with God; and with the Holy Spirit; and the Word of God for guidance and strength in the fruit and giftedness to which God has called them! Dr. Jay R. Leach

A habit for a life-time

Educators tell us it takes about thirty consecutive days to make a habit stick. Constant repetition is awkward at first; however, it becomes second nature once the habit is formed. Good habits are harder to form than bad habits simply because bad habits come naturally. We all need to form good habits, but for the Christian the priority should be the habit of godliness. It is in the Word of God that the habit of godliness is formed. There are no short-cuts to forming the habit of godliness. The Scriptures are to be lived in for a life-time; just as if they were your home. In these perilous times, there is no better place to live.

Five marks for the believer

In 2 Timothy 3:14-17, the apostle Paul puts forth five marks of the believer who lives in the Scriptures as outlined below:

1. Scripture must be [lived] in (v. 14).
2. Scripture makes the believer [wise] to salvation (v. 15).
3. Scripture is [inspired] by God (v. 16).
4. Scripture is [profitable] to the believer (v. 16).
5. Scripture [perfects] the believer and equips him or her for every good work (v. 17).

The Word of God will keep you from sin or – sin will keep you from the Word of God!

In the remainder of this chapter we will spend some time expanding on the outline:

Live in the Scriptures (v. 14).

As a Bible teacher I often hear people say, "They know the Word – they just won't live or apply it!" Believers are to live meaningful lives as they dwell in the Scriptures. The apostle Paul wanted his young student Timothy to understand that it's not enough:

- To have learned the Scriptures.
- To be assured that the teachings of the Scriptures are true.
- To know that your teacher is teaching the truth.

One day I went to an agent seeking an appraisal on a house we owned. He came out to take measurements, but he only examined the outside and the living room. The appraiser wanted to complete his work on an assumption for the rest of the house.

Over the years Magdalene and I made many improvements to the house and property; so, without seeing the inside for himself his assessment would at best be an estimated guess. But to truly know the house he would have to examine all of it as if he was going to live there himself.

Note the word "continue" in verse 14, it means to abide, to remain, to live in, and to stay in the Scriptures. How did that relate to Timothy and to every believer? Timothy had to live in the Scriptures – live, move, and have his being in the Scriptures. Not only that, he had to live out the Scriptures – continue to walk and live in the truths of the Scriptures. He had to do what the Scriptures said. We have to do likewise!

The Scriptures will make you wise (v. 15).

The Scriptures can make a man [or woman] wise unto salvation. This is the message of verse 15. The Holy Scriptures can save a person and his or her world. How? Through faith in Jesus Christ and His "finished work" on Calvary. The Holy Scriptures alone tell us,

"That God so loved the world, that He gave His only begotten Son, that whosoever believes in Him shall not perish, but will have eternal life" (John 3:16):

- God sent His Son into the world to reveal and tell the truth.
- Jesus lived a perfect life and secured the perfect righteousness – that when a person believes in Him, God takes that person's faith and counts it to his righteousness.
- Jesus took all the sins of humanity upon Himself and bore the penalty and punishment of those sins. Additionally, He died for humanity – that when a person believes in Jesus Christ, God counts his or her faith as having died in Christ and thereby he or she will never die.
- Jesus was raised from the dead to live eternally in the presence of the Father; that when a person believes in Jesus Christ, God takes that person's faith and counts it as the resurrection of Jesus Christ. That person is counted as having been raised and given eternal life.

The bottom line is: The Scriptures tell us how we can be saved through God's only begotten Son. Living in the Word of God confirms, the only wisdom that can save the world – the wisdom of God found only in His Holy Word, the Bible (see John 20:31).

The Scriptures are inspired by God (v. 16a).

Today, extremists in secularism, progressivism and conservatism are attempting to change or adjust the Word of God to fit their own pleasures and lifestyles. It is imperative that they come to realize the Bible was given to us by God and not human beings. Scripture is inspired by God; which means God-breathed. The idea here is that God breathed out the Scripture or produced them the way He did the Creation. The assurance of accuracy and dependability of Scripture is easily seen in what the Scripture has to say on the subject:

- The Holy Spirit is the author of the Scripture (see 2 Peter 1:19-21; John 116:12-15; 1 Corinthians 2:9-10).
- The writers of the Old Testament affirm the Bible is the Word of God (see Isaiah 8:1;1, 11; Jeremiah 1:9; 5:14; 7:27; Micah 3:8).

- The writers of the New Testament affirm the Bible is the Word of God (Acts 15:28; 1 Corinthians 2:13; 3:1; 11:23; 14:37; 2 Peter 3:2; Galatians 1:11-12; 1 Thessalonians 2:13).
- Jesus affirms that the Bible is the Word of God (see Mark 7_ 6-13; John 10:35; Luke 4:4; 24:25-27; John 16:13).

"For this reason, we also thank God without ceasing, because when you received the Word of God which you heard from us, you welcomed it not as the word of men, but as it is in truth, the Word of God, which also effectively works in you who believe" (1 Thessalonians 2:13).

Paul was continually thankful for the salvation of the Thessalonians who had welcomed the Word of God. Their salvation was completed by the Spirit when they put their faith in Christ. Note the balance of the Spirit and the Word. Therefore, they could contrast the Word of God, with its transforming effect, on the immoral pagan religions which only further perverted the people.

The Word without the Spirit is lifeless; it has no power to act. Likewise, the work of the Holy Spirit is always in tandem with the work of the Word to convict the believer of the truth.

The Scriptures are profitable to the Christian (v. 16b).

The word is profitable meaning it is useful, beneficial and helpful. Therefore, we can conclude that God gave the Bible to humanity to help them. Four very specific helps found in the Bible stand out:

1. The Bible is profitable for **doctrine** – God wants all humanity to have a biblical worldview. The Bible gives a person the principles and precepts for righteous and godly living; and it gives them the doctrines and foundations for life. Jesus said, *"You search the Scriptures, for in them you think you have eternal life: and these are they which testify of Me"* (John 5:39). The Jewish religious leaders of Jesus' day searched the Scriptures diligently, but did not see Jesus as the Messiah, nor did they believe in Him.
2. The Bible is profitable for **reproof** – God desires a person to sense conviction and to be rebuked when he or she is disobedient to

His will. The Scripture reveals God's will and the consequences of disobedience to His will (see Hebrews 4:12).

3. The Bible is profitable for **correction** – God's intent with the Bible is that mankind can be corrected when he or she is wrong. Thus, the Bible teaches obedience through discipline (see Hebrews 5:8).

4. The Bible is profitable for **instruction in righteousness** – God wants Christians to know to do right, also to think and talk right. In Titus 2:12-13, we are told how to live "soberly, righteously, and godly in this present world; looking for that blessed hope, and the glorious appearing of the great God and our Savior Jesus Christ."

Peter says, "As newborn babes, desire the sincere milk of the Word, that you may grow thereby; if so be that you have tasted that the Lord is gracious" (1 Peter 2:2-3).

The Scriptures perfect and equip the Christian (v. 17).

By the word "perfect" the writer means the Christian is complete, matured, and a Holy Spirit-filled disciple – a process which cannot happen apart from the Scriptures. Humans were created for the glory of God and they are to live by the Word of God. If one tries to live without God and His Word, he or she fails – and lives an incomplete, immature, and unfulfilled existence. This is especially true of the person who claims to be a minister or teacher of God's Word.

Spiritual Growth

I heard a story about a man who wanted to go on a five-day sea-cruise, but had little resources. He had enough money for the ticket – but worried that he would not be able to pay for his meals, he prepared and packed a five-day supply of peanut butter sandwiches for the journey. On the last day of the cruise he ran out of sandwiches, so he decided to purchase the last meal served before embarking. He was amazed at the very elaborately prepared tables of food; and the people serving themselves.

He asked the steward where he had to go to pay for his meal. The steward informed Him that there was no charge for the meal. Further he explained, breakfast, lunch, and dinner where prepared for the passengers each day of the cruise as a part of the cruise package. He was shocked when he realized, that he had missed out on the daily feasts because he settled for a peanut butter sandwich.

Many of us are surviving on peanut butter sandwiches, forfeiting the blessings of feeding at the Lord's banquet table. Only the truth of God's Word brings spiritual growth. No parent is satisfied to see a child continue to look and act like a baby once infancy is over. Neither is God satisfied to see Christians remain immature.

The writer of the Book of Hebrews said, "they were not ready for solid food yet because they were not even weaned from the milk of the truth of God's Word. Then He said,

"For everyone who partakes only on milk is unskilled in the word of righteousness, for he is a babe. But solid food belongs to those who are full age, that is those who by reason of use have their senses exercised to discern both good and bad" (Hebrews 5:13-14 ESV).

The Hebrews were regressing in their understanding concerning the Messiah. They had enough exposure to the gospel to be teaching it to others, yet they were babies, too infantile and unskilled to comprehend it, let alone, teach the truth. Jesus invited these unbelieving Jews to the salvation perfection which come only through following Him obediently in faith (Matthew 19:21 ESV).

Paul wrote that those who had come to Christ by faith were mature and able to receive the wisdom of God (1 Corinthians 2:6). He described believers as "mature" when he referred to those whose righteousness was in Christ, as opposed to those who had confidence in the flesh (Philippians 3:2-20 ESV). The one who had come to Christ for spiritual completion is:

- Trained by the Word to discern truth from error and holy behavior from unholy (2 Timothy 3:16, 17).
- A "doer of the Word, and not a hearer only" (James 1:22 ESV).
- Moved from milk of the Word to the meat of the Word – by practicing the Word.

What renders a person mature? One thing is the ability to make responsible decisions on one's own. When children do not have to be told every little thing, you know they are maturing. When they determine they are going to do it on their own – you know maturity is setting in.

Maturity comes for Christians when we can take the meat of God's Word in stronger portions and apply them to the decisions of life as our natural way of living out the Word.

The Living Word

When you see the Word of God come alive in your life, you will experience it flowing from your heart, and when you see God honor His Word – your Bible memory pays-off. Many of us have been telling the devil to go away for years. But he doesn't go anywhere, because our words mean nothing to him. Jesus is our teacher in this matter, Satan is only afraid of God's Word. Most Christians do not know that Satan can not hang with the Word. Why? Because it is the power of God (see Romans 1:16 ESV).

When Satan hears the Word, he hears the voice of God. And he can't handle that voice. Jesus quoted three verses to Satan, and he was gone (see Matthew 4). Try using the Word on the devil when he tries to destroy your life, and you will see the power of the Living Word when applied in the life of the believer. Read the Word, study it diligently, memorize it and meditate on it. The psalmist said, "My eyes anticipate the night watches that I may meditate on Thy Word" (Psalm 119:148). KJV

Joshua also demonstrates how powerful meditation really is. Joshua was the busiest man in all of Israel. The task before him was to conquer the Promised Land with its walled cities and giants. God did not give him a battle plan per se. He told Him:

This book of the law shall not depart from your mouth, but you shall meditate on it day and night, so that you may be careful to do according to all that is written in it; for then you will make your way prosperous, and then you will have success (Joshua 1:8 ESV).

Much of what we hear preached today may lead you to believe that the power of meditation means a new car or a bigger house. As the children of God, we know better than that. For us as Christians it means fulfilling God's purpose for our lives, whether that includes the car or house. To meditate may be illustrated through the eating habits of a cow.

A cow has two stomachs as it eats grass it is stored in the second stomach after a little chewing in the first stomach, later in the heat of the day the cow lays in the shade and regurgitates the grass back up and chews on it some more then finally swallows it. That is the picture of what God told Joshua and that is the picture of what God wants us to do with His Word.

The answer is in the Bible

Everything we know about God and His will comes from God's own revelation. We only know the good news of Jesus Christ because God has revealed the truth about Himself to us – and He has done that in His Word, the Bible. The truth of Christ is the means God's Spirit uses to reconcile us to Himself. New life comes through the Word, just as Jesus prayed: "I do not pray for these alone, but also for those who will believe in Me through their word" (John 17:20 ESV).

It is important that we note, belief will come *through their word*. And that is what happens throughout the New Testament. For instance, Peter preached to Cornelius and his household; and "while Peter was still speaking these words, the Holy Spirit fell upon all those who heard the word" (Acts 10:44).

God had told Cornelius through an angel to expect what just happened. Peter will "tell you words by which you and your household will be saved" (Acts 11:14 ESV). This is the reason Paul said, "Faith comes by hearing the Word of God" (Romans 10:17 ESV).

Additionally, the preached Word creates life. Not only does the preached Word create the Christian life; but it sustains and transforms it. The Bible is our lifeline, our feast. It should be our sincere desire to search out all that God has revealed about Himself in it, and then joyfully accept it, adopt it, obey it, submit ourselves to it, and enjoy God's blessings in it thoughout life. "Give Him praise and glory!"

QUESTIONS FOR DISCUSSION & REFLECTION: CHAPTER 5

1. Discuss the five marks of a Christian who lives in the Scriptures.
2. The only wisdom that can save the world is the _____ _____ _____.
3. Discuss the four specific Bible helps found in this chapter.
4. What are some of the advantages of one who receives the Word of God?
5. Discuss the destiny of one who tries to live without God and His Word.

CHAPTER SIX

PERILOUS TIMES

"This know also, that in the last days perilous times shall come" (II Timothy 3:1 ESV).

When reading through the Apostle Paul's thesis wrote to young pastor Timothy; it seems as though he was placed somewhere 2000 years ago that enabled him to peer down through the corridors of time, the future church and the national society of the United States from any city U.S.A. as they are today. His prophesy is as if he was watching our daily lives as reported on the morning and evening cultural newscasts; and conveying to Timothy what the last days of the Gentiles would be like. Listen to his commentary:

"Men will be lovers of themselves, lovers of money, boasters, proud, blasphemers, disobedient to parents, unthankful, unholy, unloving, unforgiving, slanderers, without self-control, brutal, despisers of good, traitors, headstrong, haughty, lovers of pleasure rather than lovers of God, having a form of godliness but denying the power." And from such people turn away (vv. 1-5 ESV).

These perilous times have been building through the ages and there have been comparable societies through the centuries the culmination of the last days is at hand – according to the Scripture even Satan knows the time is short! It seems that our national consciousness has been numbed. Perhaps the secular media, secular education along with secular opinion have been Satan's main weapons in this battle for the mind of America, but I think the greater blame may fall to the Christians' lack of Spiritual and biblical knowledge of the truth. Therefore, they have lost the ability to properly counter his moves and counterfeit claims with the applicable use of God's Word in all of life. The Bible says the Word is like a two-edged sword and a hammer. But the voluntary lack of Bible knowledge is spiritually overcoming and destroying this nation. Paul's exhortations in chapter two are given in context of difficult times:

- Endure hardships
- Be diligent
- Rightly divide the Word of truth
- Be a vessel fit for the Master's use

As New Testament believers, we must be striving to live out these exhortations from Paul, as satanic roadblocks and erroneous signs are strewn across our path by the rising apostates, false prophets and teachers to fill the void. However, those Christians who are in the light are alert and looking to the Lord, who told us these things would come. The wise person will heed these truths and live a godly life that counts. We are aware of Satan's devices and know that those who attempt to genuinely follow Christ are ridiculed as being bigoted, antiquated and narrow-minded – but take heart, Jesus faced the same! In Matthew 4:1-11 ESV, He countered Satan with three words ["it is written"] and Satan had to flee! What a timeless application lesson Jesus has left for us. Undoubtedly, Satan fears and flees from the Word of God; but he merely laughs at our words alone!

A Godless World

Why will the days be perilous, because the world will be godless? Many years ago, Evangelist Oliver Green made a very practical and straightforward comment on this age:

"This is an unholy age. People have lost respect for their bodies. Women (even church members, professing Christians) dress indecently and expose their nakedness. Men do the same. Men and women tear down the temple of the Holy Spirit.

"What? Know ye not that your body is the temple of the Holy Ghost which is in you, which ye have of God, and ye are not your own? For ye are bought with a price: therefore, glorify God in your body, and in your spirit, which are God's" (1 Corinthians 6:19-20). KJV

"A person who tears down and destroys his [or her] body through drink, tobacco, foods, other addictions and habits is unholy in his [or her] living. "This is an age when people have lost respect and reverence for a Holy God, the Holy Bible and holy living. He went on to say, "If you are a 'good mixer,' if you play cards [social media] dance, drink, dress indecently, laugh at filthy jokes, you are a wonderful fellow, a number one citizen, and you can teach a Sunday school class, pray in public, sing in the choir, and hold several responsible positions in the church. But the church member who refuses to drink cocktails, use tobacco [and drugs], attend parties, and who believes in old-time Christianity is called a fanatic or a religious square."[15] [brackets added].

Wild perverse behavior and rejection of God and His righteousness mark our day. Perilous times mean difficult, troublesome, trying, hard, violent, threatening, and dangerous days. It is important to note, that the marks of the end time are somewhat characteristic of all ages – however, Scripture leaves no doubt about what is to come as the perils are intensified in the last days (see Matthew 24:1-25; 46 ESV).

We can make a difference

We are the people of God [salt and light] who can make a difference. But rather than do so, Jesus said most Christians in our day would become so wrapped up in their own everyday lives; they would be of little use to the kingdom of heaven. Narcissism, materialism and consumerism have so engaged the average Christian that he or she is so busy buying, selling, building, planting, and marrying that they ignore all the warning signs and the fruit such societal living produces.

The signs are clearly visible everywhere that America is on the brink of a great chastening or a retributive judgment from the hand of God. This year 2021 is no different than the previous four when considering disasters. However, the disasters get more intense and a lot more unfamiliar, case in point, the COVID-19 is still raging after twelve months, with no end in sight. The recent tornado in Alabama seems to have just popped up. In 2019 Hurricane Dorian's damage is still being accessed. In 2018 many people paid little attention to early warnings climaxing in much confusion as was played out in hurricanes Florence and Micheal; and other disasters have caught many people by surprise, as they began to relax and go back to their usual routines, just to be caught up isn the next disaster. Many people are still homeless from 2017's hurricane Matthew. Sadly, so many lost everything they owned; and many lives were lost. Nearly 500,000 lives have been lost to the COVDID-19 in the U.S. as of 1/20/21.

On the West coast, California has experienced a couple of earthquakes; at the same time wrestling with COVID-19 and record setting fires creating the worst air to breathe in the world. Daily thunder storms, devastating hurricanes, tornados tear through our southern and midwestern states, new weather records are being set east to west and north to south all across this land. As I write three blizzards are streached for the Midwest to the Northeast. What new catastophies will result around the world as a result of the great smoke from the fires? Recent catastrophic, security breaches in "trusted" personal and corporate data at all levels are hacked by known assailants. Everywhere the technological cloud grows larger, more bizarre, and unknown day by day. Numerous murders make it seem that the populance places little or no value on human lives today. Today on the news, a son was charged with the 1st degree murder of his biological father.

However, these tragedies are dwarfed when compared to the catastrophic harm secularism, materialism, and consumerism flowing into the vacuum created at foundation levels of the entire nation, spearheaded by the subtle deconstruction of modernism for postmodernism.

These are truly perilous times however; nothing should surprise Christians, because it was prophesied in Scripture two thousand years ago. Can the fires in our Western States and the long-lasting but now mostly forgotten eruption of the Kilauea volcano in Hawaii serve as a reminder that Hell[16] is a reality? It was reported in the news last week that Kilauea has come back to Life.

Although there are many religions to day that say it does not exist? Yet, they admit people will spend eternity somewhere (?). Perhaps it will be a reminder for all who saw the frightening lava [2000 plus degrees Fahrenheit] flowing on the news for days. Then there are the present-day fires in California and other Western States [with fire tornados]; however, all should realize that even those do not equate to the *"lake of fire"* into which the false prophet and Antichrist will spend eternity with Satan, his demons, and all unbelievers whom Jude said, *"Have gone the way of Cain"* (Jude 11). The way of Cain is the way of pride and self-righteousness (see Genesis 4:3-8; Hebrews 11:4; 1 John 3:12).

Even hell itself shall one day be cast into the lake of fire. And even though hell was not created for humanity, all those persons who reject Christ and His work on Calvary will spend eternity there. Universalism, the belief in "no hell" and "all will be saved" is on the rise. When I entered the Army in the late 50's, there were two recognized religions on the tombstones of America's fallen soldiers: Protestants [the Cross] or Jews [the Star of David]. Research has shown some 225 different emblems representing the different belief systems today.

Could the moving of the United States Embassy several years ago to Jerusalem and the ensuing border problems be a "wake-up" call for the world to refocus on the Word of God and what matters most?

In the Old Testament people rejected God. In the New Testament people rejected Christ. In this generation people have rejected the Holy Spirit.
Jay R. Leach

Keep looking up!

Look up saints, for the fulfillment of Jesus' promise to come back for a church without a spot or wrinkle. Isn't it imminent? Are you Rapture ready? The truth of the matter is, today all Christians must have faith, pray, teach, give, and witness the gospel at every opportunity. The Scriptures command us to do so whether the people listen or not. Pastors, churches, and families must prioritize the study of God's Word. We must preach the true gospel of Christ, for "It is the power of God unto salvation" (Romans 1:16). The power of the Word of God brings new life.

Those who study will readily see many strange things we are experiencing today that – Christ Himself predicted. Is the rapture on the horizon? Who will be in heaven because you cared enough to give them the gospel? Who will be in hell because we didn't care enough to share the gospel with them? Biblically speaking the Gentile nations are in turmoil and we've almost reached the point of worldwide confusion even hearing the clamor for the Antichrist?

`It is noted, nations and religions cause wars; so many people think that getting rid of borders and all religions will solve that problem. The one world government and one world religion of the Antichrist is coming. However, what the world really desires, only Christ Himself can provide, He promised that He would return and make things right – and He will!

Who or what is vicious today?

On one of the Wild Kingdom TV show one Saturday morning I saw a man playing with a very poisonous puff adder snake allowing it to crawl up his leg and arm – he stated that the snake will not become aggressive and bite unless you do something like squeeze it or step on it. Do you believe that? Later, on the same show another man risked his life by walking into a pride of lions to wrestle-play with its leader, an adult male lion that was raised in captivity and later released back into the wild. Are we as human beings trading places with the animals in viciousness?

At the same time consider the human beings who are so viciously evil that they will fire a gun into a crowd of people aiming to wound or kill one person whom they think has offended them. Many crimes are boldly committed today simply in the name of boredom. Thieves boldly break into homes and businesses knowing that security cameras are recording their every move; many of them seem to defy logic by posing or dancing unmasked for the cameras.

For some time, the nation of Israel was being systematically worked out of much of the equation as a favored nation – even though they are without a doubt our best and most supportive ally in the Middle East. Thank the Lord that has changed. We can add to that our own downward spiral as a nation; and rejection of God along with His promises to Abraham concerning Israel and the Gentile nations.

No longer debtors

The Apostle Paul not only wanted to assure the Roman Christians that they

are no longer obligated to the flesh, to yield to its suggestions; but he reminds them of where such life leads – to death! He is saying to believers today as he said to the believers of that day, "Brethren we are not debtors to the flesh, to live habitually under the domination of the flesh:

- Joining in the world's deadly philosophies and raising them up against the knowledge of God and holding the souls of people captive (Carefully study 2 Corinthians 10:3-5 ESV).
- The present Satanic world systems are temporary; and in a continual process of disintegration – heading for destruction (see Romans 8:18-22 ESV).
- In contrast to these systems God's will is permanent and unchangeable.

Sin is a sickness and Jesus is its cure!
Billy Graham

Therefore, if you are living so; you are dying. "But if you are habitually putting to death the deeds of the flesh – you will live." The Apostle John exhorts,

"Do not love the world or the things in the world. If anyone loves the world, the love of the Father is not in him. For all that is in the world – the lust of the flesh, the lust of the eyes, and the pride of life – is not of the Father but is of the world. And the world is passing away, and the lust of it; but he who does the will of God abides forever" (I John 2:15-17 ESV).

God, not the world must have the first place in the Christian's life. This is not a reference to the physical world, but the invisible spiritual systems of evil and all that it offers in opposition to God, His Word, and His people. While the world's philosophies, and ideologies and many other things offered may appear attractive and appealing, that is a gross deception. It's true and pervasive nature is evil, harmful, ruinous, and satanic.

The apostle Paul uses Ancient Israel's forty-year journey between Egypt and Canaan to serve as a sober warning of the misuse of freedom, the dangers of overconfidence and the lack of self-control on the journey. The Israelites:

- misused their new-found freedom,
- fell into idolatry, immorality,
- and disqualified themselves from the Lord's blessings.

As the times passes the hyper-grace and happy church crowds are increasing in great numbers around America as people are deceived by false teaching concerning sin and grace. Such activities lead people to no longer reverence or fear God.

Paul often used the metaphor of an athlete or that of a soldier who failed to meet basic training requirements, they could not participate at all, much less – have an opportunity to win.

Made by the Holy Spirit

Paul may be especially referring to such fleshly sins that disqualify a person from preaching and leading the church, particularly being blameless and above reproach. The Scripture says,

Mine eyes shall be upon the faithful of the land, that they may dwell with me, he that walketh in a perfect way, he shall serve me (Psalm 101:6 ESV).

A bishop then must be blameless, the husband of one wife, vigilant, sober, of good behavior, given to hospitality, apt to teach (1 Timothy 3:2 ESV).

If any be blameless, the husband of one wife, having faithful children not accused of riot or unruly (Titus 1:6)

Those who obey, abide, and follow His will are His people forever. While God offers eternal life to His children, the present age is doomed (see 1 Corinthians 7:31; 2 Corinthians 4:18 ESV).

The cost of silence

The philosophy that there is more than one way [Jesus Christ] to God is gaining momentum among many carnal Christians. The old folks use to say, *"it's better "telt" than "felt!"* Of course, I am referring to the true Gospel of Jesus Christ. We hear much today about different "paths" which suggests a search for one among many; also, a path is something we strive to find and work out ourselves. Yet, the true way, Jesus Christ, is closer to you than the nose on your face (see Jeremiah 29:13 ESV).

Don't be deceived by the many who are speaking, no matter their financial status, or social standing. Unless their answer is Jesus Christ, whatever they offer leads to nowhere. Instead, turn to Jesus Christ and receive the hope and forgiveness He alone can give. Only Christ could say,

> *"I am the way*
> *and*
> *the truth*
> *and*
> *the life.*
> *No one comes*
> *to the Father*
> *except*
> *through Me."*
> John 14:6 ESV

I will close this chapter with a familiar illustration: "If you had possession of the only cure for a certain type of cancer." You would no doubt do everything you could to convince people to take it. The same holds true with Jesus Christ. The Bible speaks of the deadly disease called sin. Like a cancer sin attacks and pollutes our lives and twists our minds – but worse it cuts us off from God and from heaven. Is there a cure for sin? Yes! God has given us the only cure, Jesus Christ, His only begotten Son, who gave His life for us:

For God so loved the world, that He gave His only begotten Son, that whosoever believeth in Him should not perish, but have everlasting life (John 3:16). KJV

QUESTIONS FOR DISCUSSION & REFLECTION: CHAPTER 6

1. Define perilous times from Paul's explanation in chapter 6.
2. Generally, contrast Paul's vision of the last days as compared to the United States today.
3. Discuss the decline of Bible Reading in the United States and its impact on our culture today.
4. Discus the passing of time as it pertains to the last days.
5. What did Paul mean by "putting to death the deeds of the flesh?"

CHAPTER SEVEN

AS IN THE DAYS OF NOAH

"And God saw that the wickedness of man was great in the earth, and that every imagination of the thoughts of his heart was only evil continually" (Genesis 6:5).

God created humans for His glory, but He created them free moral agents – therefore each person can choose his or her own destiny. Thus, we have a world rebelling not only against God's fundamental decencies, but against God Himself! God's assessment in Noah's day was, *"the wickedness of man was great in the earth, and .... every imagination of the thoughts of man's heart was evil continually .... and the earth was filled with violence."*

Imagination

What people are and, what the world is to them depend totally on the concepts they set up for their inner eyes to see and obey. As a man *"thinks in his heart so is he"* (Proverbs 23:7). Imagination creates its images, and those images can become idols that take the place of God. The fail-safe way to keep them out is to make sure that God comes in! This thinking has caused some generations in the past to look unfavorably toward the use of imagination.

An Eastern proverb says, "The great teacher is the one who turns your ears into eyes, so you can see the truth."

The only deterrent against corrupt thoughts is to fill the mind and heart continually with wholesome godly thoughts. Think on things above!

Remember Jesus' parable of the house swept, garnished and left *empty,* being invaded by seven devils worse than the ones that had been driven out" (see Luke 11:21-24-26).

When imagination ceases to dwell upon the great convictions of God's Spirit and Word – debasing progressivism, secularism, materialism, and various other isms so easily overcome us. Whether Psychology agrees or not; biblically-speaking, evil and wickedness cannot be overcome by the dispensing of more drugs, medical arguments or political correctness – according to the Scripture, evil *must be* overcome by good! Paul admonishes,

"I find then a law, that, when I would do good, evil is present with me, the one who wills to do good. For I delight in the law of God according to the inward man. But I see another law in my members, warring against the law of my mind, and bringing me into captivity to the law of sin which is in my members. **O wretched man that I am! Who will deliver me from this body of death? I thank God – through Jesus Christ our Lord! So then with with the mind I myslf serve the law of God, but with the flesh the law of sin** (Romans 7:21-25). KJV.

This passage of Scripture should be a "Wake up call" and help to many Christians who are trying to go it on their own strength. I lived in chapter seven for a number of years not realizing I was under the law [in self-life]. Like Paul, I cried out for deliverance. Who will deliver me from this body of death? Truly I had a saving relationship with the Lord before I left home for the Army. However, like kids going off for college, I was in for a culture shock. The battle raged within me and I succumbed to the law of sin. I heard a Bible teacher say, "Just like you did not *save* yourself; you cannot *keep* yourself!" He further spoke of our new divine nature no longer sides with sin – but joyfully agrees with the law of God again. "Therefore, there is no condemnation...." (Romans 8:1). The devil could no longer beat me over the head with my past, I was justified! Jesus paid the penalty for the verdict demanded. Therefore, "there is no condemnation" for those "in Christ Jesus" – *who walk not according to the flesh, but walk after the Spirit.* Who delivered me from this body of sin? The Holy Spirit! (Study prayerfully Romans 1-8; John 14:15-18, 26; 15:1-11; 16:1-15; Galatians 5:1-26; Jude 24 ESV).

It is dangerous to be the kind of Christian who listens to biblical teaching but does not go and live out what they were taught. The Bible says such a person has been "deceived!"

James warns us, "Do not merely listen to the Word, and so deceive yourselves." Do what it says! Anyone who listens to the Word but does not do what it says is like a man [or woman] who looks at his [or her] face in a mirror and, after looking, goes away and immediately forgets what he or she looks like. But the person who looks intently into the perfect law of liberty and continues in it and is not a forgetful hearer but a doer of the work, this one will be blessed in what he does" (James 1:22-25). Emphasis added. God works through people who are willing to obey His Word. The Lord has declared, "This is the one I esteem: he [or she] who is humble and contrite in spirit, and trembles at my Word" (Isaiah 66:2 ESV). [bracket is mine]

Make it real

There are so many pseudo religious-Christian activities going on in the name of the Lord today that have absolutely none of His power or presence at its center. Numerous sermons are preached every week in churches around America and the world, that are full of man's wisdom but totally devoid of the anointing and power of the Holy Spirit.

Such "work" is never acceptable to the kingdom of God. So many Christians think it takes more human qualifications such as titles, degrees, and political clout to serve the LORD. It is much better to simply re-commit yourself to Him and ask the Lord to use you for His glory.

The Bible states clearly the qualifications for serving God:

> *He has showed you, O man what is good.*
> *And what does the Lord require of you?*
> *To act justly and to love mercy*
> *and to walk humbly with your God.*
> Micah 6:8 ESV

I remember and old anointed preacher in my childhood that we [children] loved to hear preach and teach. When he would say, "let me frame it up for you." We knew it was going to be good. In his framing he fired our imagination with vivid word pictures, revealing the unknown through analogies; which produced clarity and retention of the message. His words created mental images of the texts more than 70 years ago that remain me with me to this day.

It is time for more Christians to imitate the church father, Augustine, history records that he would read the Gospels in the morning and then, go out in the afternoon and put into action what he had read. When he read of how Jesus washed the feet of His disciples, Augustine washed the feet of his brothers in Christ.

When Peter and John appeared before the Sanhedrin, the Pharisees could not understand how these two unlearned ordinary men could speak with such authority; they took note that, "they had been with Jesus" (Acts 4:13 ESV). Today God continues to use ordinary people for His glory.

Retribution

The world in rebellion against God brings *retribution*. There can be a point of disintegration due to evil – then the forces of good and morality are not strong enough to hold back the pressure of moral *consequences*. The past one-hundred years of the History of Western Civilization attests to that reality.

It would rain upon the earth not only for forty days as in the days of Noah – World Wars I and II, Korea, Vietnam, Iraq and our constant military interventions around the globe [the longest one still on going in the Middle East], dragging through decades of war spreading its slime of bitterness and suffering. The flood is not water only, but now in every reoccurring judgment it is, of blood and tears (see Amos 4).

Noah's neighbors are here today

The Biblical truth of the flood and Noah building the ark has been down-graded almost to fairy-tale status; at the same time the "rain bow" of the covenant God established with all the earth has been made the symbol of the LBGTQ community. Have you seen a rainbow in the sky lately? As a child, it seems that rainbows were the usual occurrence once the afternoon thunderstorm storm had passed. The old saying spoke of a treasure at the end of the rainbow.

I would chase after it but never reach the end! However, while humanity grows in doubt of its validity; the vast mountain chains and rocks cry out around the globe the vivid reality of the past flood of [judgment]. The ark has many parallels in these last days.

Perhaps the gigantic irony today is that the colleges and universities of this nation – the very institutions that are intended to educate and intellectually challenge the people – often introduce environments that are constantly accused of being one-sided and biased:

- After all, college is intended to be an intensive time of self-exploration, a time in which *young people* in a sense are opened to the world around them, with many different perspectives and experiences *helping to **shape** their contextual understandings.*
- Yet, in contrast, higher education today is often a breeding ground for exclusively progressive and extreme conservtive ideals and values *concealed, paraded, and marketed* **to young people** as unadulterated truth.
- Unfortunately, young people are constantly fed this information by professors from the left and right fringes who inject their worldview in the classroom with little regard or need for *different beliefs* in the educational marketplace.

- These professors' ideals presented as truth are many times so filtered that *opposing views* are either down-graded into silence or ignored entirely.
- Therefore, their progressive or conservative views are often pervasive and treated as gospel when in fact they're nothing more than mere opinions.
- Really devastating is the fact that from the beginning in pre-school an environment in which young people are given an imbalanced perspective on *key* religious, social, political, and international issues, or one in which those with a balanced perspective are too afraid to share their views with colleagues for fear of reprisal.

This bias against Christians is bearing evil fruit; for example, statistics show that any Christian professor has a distinctive disadvantage going for a job in academia. It's easy to see that Christianity, God, and Christian values have been marginalized in today's university systems.

The Noah parallel

I'm sure that Noah was the laughing stock of his day, as he went about building his ark and preaching "it's going to rain" and "the flood is coming" for 120 years. Especially, since up to that time it had never rained! Noah was building that ark because a *crisis* was at hand. If the people had only listened there would have probably been more than one ark. It was not necessarily that they did not know that *deserved* judgment was coming, but they ignored it – many are treating COVID-19 in the same manner. Note the following scriptural references:

- They had the promise of *"the first gospel"* (Genesis 3:15 ESV).
- They had the record of God killing animals to provide a *sacrificial* covering for Adam and Eve (Genesis 3:8, 9, 21).
- They had the witness of Abel *"brought the first born of his flock"* (Genesis 4:4 ESV).
- They had the witness of Enoch, *"Who walked with God; and he was not, for God took him"* (Genesis 5:24 ESV).
- They had the witness of the Spirit for the LORD said, *"My Spirit shall not strive with man forever...."* (Genesis 6:3-4 ESV). Here we have sexual immorality which has brought deserved judgment throughout the Scriptures (also study carefully Genesis 19:4-8).

"The earth also was corrupt before God, and the earth was filled with violence. So, God looked upon the earth, and indeed it was corrupt; for all flesh had corrupted their way on the earth. And God said to Noah, "The end of all flesh has come before Me, for the earth is filled with violence through them; and behold, I will destroy them with the earth" (Genesis 611-14 ESV).

They had the witness of Noah, *"But Noah found grace in the eyes of the LORD"* (Genesis 6:8 ESV).

Noah preached and warned them of the impending judgment for 120 years, but they only shrugged their shoulders in passing. This is generally what people have done down through the ages since.

"In the days that were before the flood," said Jesus, *"they were eating and drinking, marrying, and giving in marriage … until the flood came, and took them all away"* (Matthew 24:38-39 NKJV)

The Assyrians are coming

"Woe to them that are at ease in Zion," cried the prophet (Amos 6:1) to

the arrogant people of Israel which did not believe that the destruction by Assyria was coming – it came in less than a generation. "I set a watchman over you." Jeremiah preached in the name of God, "saying Hearken to the sound of the trumpet. But they said, "We will not hearken" (Jeremiah 6:17 NKJV).

Not even when the Babylonians were at their gate! *"My people are destroyed for lack of knowledge,"* cried Hosea (4:6 NKJV). They lacked the knowledge because they were too overly satisfied doing their own thing to want to know. What a *cultural* commentary – "they don't want to know!" Isn't that true of the United States and the West today?

Many times, people stare so hard at what they want to see that they totally miss seeing the realities. *"You know how to interpret the appearances in the sky,* Jesus said, *"But you cannot interpret the signs of the times"* (Matthew 16:3 NKJV). Noah's neighbors looked at the ordinary skies that seemed to promise another season of beautiful weather – yet they did not see in the skies of descending morality, the signs that spoke of imminent winds of judgment on the horizon.

The Western world, particularly Europe, Canada, and the United States are more like Noah's neighbors than like Noah. They eat and drink and rise to play while the storm clouds gather on the horizon (1 Corinthians 10:7 NKJV).

Walking with God

Perhaps the question will arise, how did Noah perceive what others were so blind to see? God said to Noah, *"the end of all flesh is come before me."* When you read and examine the narrative the truth is presented concretely, as if God was there standing face to face with Noah and spoke to him alone. However:

- God was speaking through the *unmistakable signs of the times* to everybody! Can't we see the same thing happening all around us today? Why are we ignoring the signs?
- But Noah was the *one* who could hear – because he was a just man and walked with God. Many times, in writing or speaking we want to note a distinction between people or things. In verse 9, God made such a distinction between Noah and all others in his generation. To do so God said he was a *just man perfect* which means he was *"genuinely righteous"* in contrast to *all* others.

In the Vietnam War, at one point, I had only one committed and active Christian in my platoon and some carnal Christians including myself. He had only been with us about a month but became a nuisance to all trying to turn our hearts to God. Though he was the lowest ranking person in the platoon, he had everybody's attention one way or the other.

One night our position came under a heavy rocket attack; when the smoke cleared, I was shocked to see that I had lost one man in the attack, it was the Christian soldier! For the rest of my tour, I was perplexed over the death of this righteous man. A few months later, I shipped back to the States. I attended church and asked the pastor, "Why did God take this young man – the only really true Christian among us!"

His answer got my full attention, he said, "He was probably the only one of you that was ready to go!" Wham! Why didn't I see that? I certainly wasn't ready. I repented of my sins and turned back to God.

In these perilous times how many leaders of the nations, and churches as well, can it be said? "He or she discerns the signs of the times and is "just and walking with God," as Noah?" Noah had no doubt never experienced rain or a flood, but he believed God and obediently moved by faith on what was revealed to him.

He heeded God's warnings by acting on his *faith* which saved him and his family not only from the deluge but also from God's judgment. Thus, he became an *"heir of the righteousness which is according to faith"* (Hebrews 11:7 NKJV).

How many of us are "just" and "walking with God?" – Who will help us to see the evils of godlessness, pride and power, and make us know that if these elements keep building up, they will bring some new floods of dreadful retribution?

- Is your family as important to you as Noah's was to him?
- Are you warning the people?
- What are you doing as a church?

Knowing and doing

Taking another look at Noah, three qualities standout, which we would do well to borrow and practice:

1. Noah *foresaw* the coming judgment.
2. He *did* something about it.
3. He *did* it ahead of time.

He began to build his ark before there was ever any obvious evidence that it would be needed. The fearful dull apathy which has made great men and women *act stupid* in matters of national safety in the past seems to have taken a hold of this nation. How clear is this to God's people? What are we doing about the apostate crisis in the United States? Noah moved by faith and built the ark according to specifications which God had given to him. Men, are you building your lives and families according to God's specifications, as recorded in His Word? Pastors are you leading your churches in obedience to the Lord's commandment to "make disciples?"

The New Testament Ark [a likeness]

The Church model is like the Ark of Noah. Just as the Ark was worth saving – not for the sake of the unclean animals:

- They almost took up all the space.
- They mostly made noise and confusion.

But it was worth saving for that small group of *rationality* that undoubtedly was as much distressed by the stench within the ark, as by the deluge raging on the outside. For the church to be the saving *remnant* it needs continual purity of doctrine and individual consecration within; "O Lord begin with me!"

The church is purified by individuals filled with the Holy Spirit and enabled by Him and the Word to be their best in the fellowship [koinonia] of the brethren. The remnant in the church like the little group in the ark would probably have become discouraged if they had not the *"one another ministries" to depend on!*

Men and women who morally and spiritually may be near discouragement are often encouraged and kept steadfast by the courage of others who face the same difficulties they face every day. They share the same assurance of hope – "Christ is coming back for His people!"

The faithfulness of God

When we seem lost to everyone and everything, we have the assurance that

we are not lost to God! The Scripture says, *"And God remembered Noah ...."* (Genesis 8:1 NKJV). Visualizing the Genesis narrative, one might suppose that Noah may have thought himself forgotten. Though he could remember that God had once spoken to him and given him His promise of protection, but where is God now?

Gazing out the window upon the empty water and sky there may seem to be no hope! Many people in times of stress and trouble have found themselves cut loose from their moorings and drifting, soon all that is familiar is gone in a world from which God Himself has left – that is, so far as they see it!

**God has not forgotten you – during this pandemic.
He is faithful to His promises. Trust Him in every circumstance
– He knows your name!
Jay R. Leach**

The flood which has carried them away; loneliness, sorrow, fear, or moral perplexity has meant only disappointment which will probably end in despair. They will say with the psalmist,

"I am so troubled that I cannot speak," and *"Is His mercy clean gone forever? Does His promise fail for everyone?"* (Psalm 77:4, 8 NKJV).

Oh! "But praise God," that is not how this story of Noah and the remnant ends. One day the deluge did cease, and the flood waters did go away. The mountaintop of hope did appear, and one day the earth was habitable again. Similarly, true Christian men and women of the church in every generation have discovered at last that God did remember and that His purposes would not fail. The reason for such faith may seem to flicker when the wind blows on the dark days – but even then, the true heart by faith knows that God is there.

In the life of the true believer, things hoped for [though not visible] are made genuine by faith. Faith is the sure foundation of things hoped for, the conviction that things hoped for are already a reality even though we do not yet, hold them in our hands. During these perilous days of mass confusion, turbulence, violence and wickedness, Christians have an anchor – Jesus Christ!

A sure anchor for the soul

In the sixth chapter of the Book of Hebrews the writer exhorted the Hebrew Christians to move on and grow in the knowledge of our Lord and Savior, Jesus Christ – God had set aside the old way:

- Christians should take heed and receive the sure Anchor today in this time of uncertainty. Our hope is embodied in Christ Himself who has entered God's presence in the Holy of Holies on our behalf.

- God's word does not need confirmation from someone else. It is a sure thing because God is faithful.
- People confirm their oaths by appealing to someone greater especially to [God] as a witness. No one is greater than God, so He can provide an oath from Himself.
- By doing so He is willingly accommodating Himself to human beings because of the unreliability of human promises (Hebrews 6:16-18 NKJV).

Two immutable things

God promises two immutable things. Immutable describes a legal will; which is unchangeable to anyone but the maker of the will. God's Christ became our Jesus and as the Man Christ Jesus, "He died on the cross for our sins. He was buried, He rose again according to the Scriptures" (I Corinthians 15:3, 4 NKJV). and He ascended to the right hand of the majesty on high, where He sits today to hear the cries of all who have fled to Him for refuge.

"Which hope we have as an anchor of the soul, both sure and steadfast, and which entered the veil; where the forerunner is for us entered, even Jesus made a high priest forever after the order of Melchizedek."

Christ is our hope

Certainly, Christ is our hope. As stated earlier, He now sits at the right hand of the Majesty. Christ is set before *all men* in the Gospel of God's great grace, and in the Gospel, we find the only hope for sinners (Romans 1:16 NKJV). In Romans 3:24, 25 NKJV we read, "Being justified freely by His grace through the redemption that is *in* Christ Jesus: Whom God has set forth to be a propitiation *through faith in His blood,* to declare His righteousness for the remission of sins that are past, through the forbearance of God."

In Galatians 3:1 Paul said, "O foolish Galatians, who has bewitched you, that you should not obey the truth, before whose eyes Jesus Christ has been evidently set forth, and crucified among you?" In the Gospel, Christ is presented to humankind as Savior – the *only* object of saving faith, the *only* object of living hope.

We noticed that the anchor of the believer is both *sure* and *steadfast* – so again we are reminded of the double immutability of God's promise. Greek scholars inform us that:

- The Greek word translated "sure" suggests that the anchor is not liable to failure that is, the anchor is so designated – large enough, heavy enough – to hold without fail, a sure guarantee it will never drift!
- The Greek word translated "steadfast" also denotes that it is impossible for the anchor to break under even the most severe storm and strain.

The sure and steadfast anchor of the soul is fastened – not to the things of the earth, but to Him who entered within the veil. The anchors dropped from a ship [4 each] goes down in the sea and fastens itself in to the ground, the bottom of the sea – but it is possible for that anchor to pull loose causing the ship to drift. But the *foundation* to which the anchor of the soul is fastened in the "Most Holy Place" within the veil.

We are anchored to the one Foundation, the Solid Rock, the Lord Jesus Christ: *"For other foundation can no man lay, then that is laid, which is Jesus Christ"* (I Corinthians 3:11 NKJV).

When Jesus died on the cross, the veil was rent (torn) into from top to bottom (Matthew 27:51), and thus the holy of holies was opened to all! Before the death of Jesus, it was opened only to the high priest; and he entered once a year with *blood for the sins of the people* (Leviticus 16:2-30 NKJV). But now the holy of holies is open to every believer.

That within the veil

God the Father is within the veil with His Son by His side; and the blood of His atonement is there. Therefore, we have the assurance that our anchor holds *sure* and *steadfast*. The closing verse of this gracious chapter points us to the very throne of God in the heavenlies, "within the veil." Paul clearly states, "Where the Forerunner is for us entered."

Christ our High Priest is passed through the heavens, Jesus the Son of God (see Hebrews 4:14). The Greek word translated "forerunner" means "a pioneer or scout, one who goes before to investigate, to prepare the way, and make the way safe for those who follow." So, thank God, our Forerunner has passed through the heavens, He has ascended to the highest heaven, He is within the veil. Through His shed blood on the cross Jesus has prepared a place of eternal rest for those who believe and trust in Him! We are complete in Him, and He is the answer to our every need!

Praising God for His long-standing plan

God had a long-standing plan for man's salvation. His own Son would take on human flesh and become one of us (John 1:14 NKJV). Acting as our "merciful and faithful High Priest" – Jesus offered the perfect sacrifice of Himself for our sins (Hebrews 2:17 NKJV):

- It was His death on the cross as the perfect Lamb of God that satisfied God's justice and exemplified God's mercy.
- He is the source and means of our reconciliation to God. Praise God for His plan to save us when we could in no way possibly have saved ourselves!
- After completion of His mission on earth. Jesus returned to the right hand of His Father to continue to serve as our eternal High Priest (Hebrews 4:14-16 NKJV).

The God-Man

In His incarnation, Jesus experienced man's weakness, so He fully *understands* from experience the weakness and frailty of humanity and the power of temptation (2:18 NKJV):

- As a man, He sympathizes with us!
- As the God-Man, He serves us as our perfect, incompatible Great High Priest, representing us before the Father.

He fully understands us and can effectively minister to us as we are complete *in* Him.

Christ our Peace

For He Himself is our peace, who has made both one, and has broken down the middle wall of partition, having abolished in His flesh the enmity, that is, the law of commandments contained in ordinances, as to create in Himself one "new man" from the two, thus making peace, and that He might reconcile them both to God in one body through the cross, thereby putting to death the enmity. And He came and preached peace to you who were afar off and to those who were near. For through Him we have both access by one Spirit to the Father (I Corinthians 2:14-18 NKJV). Emphasis added.

In this passage, Paul emphatically indicates that Jesus alone is the believer's source of peace. The middle wall of separation alludes to a wall in the temple that partitioned off the Court of the Gentiles from areas accessible only to Jews. If a Gentile wandered beyond the partition, he immediately faced certain death.

Through His death on the cross, Christ tore down *the middle wall of partition* along with other Old Testament ceremonial laws, feasts, and sacrifices which uniquely separated Jews and Gentiles. Paul referred to this wall symbolically of the *social, religious,* and *spiritual separation* that kept Jews and Gentiles apart.

Who is calling the shots?

Who is calling the shots on the direction your church is going in. Why is it still debatable whether the races should worship together in the same church? Why are the spirits of systemic racism and white privillege walking so proudly and boldly across America today? Why are old antiquated laws of repression against African Americans still on the books? Why is government still passing legislation designed to further segregate already beat-down minority groups? Why do we still have separate disability for whites and African Americans in the NFL today?

Undoubtedly, there are those who simply refuse to recognize Christ's victory of bringing down the middle wall of partition on the cross. In fact, for those who do so; the wall is still standing! My family and I returned from an assignment in Seoul, Korea and purchased a home. We excitedly moved into a very nice community. The school was a block away, there was a very beautiful church around the corner. It was the dream home for our small children, large fenced backyard, a large corner lot with nice wide sidewalks. The welcome wagon ladies came around and welcomed us to the community. Sunday came, and my middle daughter and I decided to check out the church's Sunday school – as we stepped into the foyer of the church a well-dressed white man came up to us, his message was, "I'm sure you would be more comfortable worshipping in our church located at _____ avenue which we have provided for you all." I stood there dumb-founded and crushed. Later, I met the pastor of that church at a meeting where we [pastors] were gathered to plan a city-wide revival. Right! You guessed it, his church was not considered as a possible host site. Eventually, that church under a new pastor became a joy to the community and city as well. They opened a school and academy K-12 fully integrated church and ministry activities, an evangelism and welcoming program for new families moving into the community. For that old pastor after many years, the wall of partition was still up, socially! Sadly, that old spirit of separation is common in many churches of all races today for various reasons, but it ought not be.

Eleven A.M. on Sunday is the most segregated hour in America.
– Dr. Martin Luther King Jr.

God's moral law [as summarized in the Ten Commandments and written on the hearts of all men], was not abolished but incorporated into the New Testament (see Romans 2:15). However, because it reflects His own holy nature (Matthew 5:17-19), *one new man* does not exclude anyone who comes to Him – and those who are His are not spiritually distinct from one another. "New" used here refers to something completely different from what it was before:

- It means being different in kind and quality.
- It means that spiritually, the "new person" in Christ is no longer a Jew or a Gentile [which accounts for all races] – but now a Christian (see Romans 10, 12; Galatians 3:28 NKJV).
- It means that as Jews and Gentiles are brought to God through Jesus Christ, they are brought together with each other. This was accomplished by Him on the cross as He became a curse for all humanity (Galatians 3:10-13 NKJV).

- It means that Jesus took God's wrath so that divine justice was satisfied and reconciliation with God became a reality (II Corinthians 5:19-21 NKJV).

He is the answer to our every need! Give Him praise and glory!

QUESTIONS FOR DISCUSSION & REFLECTION: CHAPTER 7

1. "What people are" and "what the world is" depend upon the conceptions they set up for their inward eyes to see and obey.
2. Discuss why arguments are not sufficient to overcome evil.
3. The world in rebellion against God brings _____.
4. Noah could hear God because he was a just man who walked with God. Are you walking with God?
5. Discuss the two immutable things, that God promised concerning the anchor for our souls.

CHAPTER EIGHT

"AS IT WAS .... SO SHALL IT BE"

"But as the days of Noah were, so shall also the coming of the Son of man be. For as in the days that were before the flood, they were eating and drinking, marrying and giving in marriage, until the day that Noah entered the ark, and did not know until the flood came, and took them all away, so also will the coming of the Son of man be" (Matthew 24:37-39).

Jesus is coming again! This is the truest fact in the universe, even surer than death, for when He comes there will be some who will never die but will be changed. How would we like to know the exact time of His coming? That question has interested believers ever since His second coming was announced. Despite the Bible's definite warning against date settings, only to be proven wrong; all sorts of foolish unscriptural guesses have been made and dates have been set.

A few years ago, I read a article about some people who gave away their personal belongings, sold their homes, and quit their jobs following a date setter. The national media carried the story for that preacher and so publicized it until it was followed on all the major networks. Of course, he was wrong. Of this type of incident, Jesus Himself says:

"But of that day and hour knows no man, no, not the angels of heaven, but My Father only" (Matthew 24:36 NKJV).

Despite this statement by Jesus; the foolish attempts of many to set dates in *utter disregard* of this warning is unbelievable. Most people have lost all interest in the return of Christ, ignoring the fact that while we cannot set the exact time of Christ's return, we may nevertheless know the approximate time of His coming again by His Spirit and the Word of God.

The Bible carries many prophetic warnings to watch for through the signs of the times, [indications of the nearness of His return]. Paul tells us in the Scripture:

"But concerning the times and the seasons, brethren, you have no need that I should write unto you. For you know perfectly that the day of the Lord so comes as a thief in the night. For when they say, "Peace and safety!" then sudden destruction comes upon them, as labor pains upon a pregnant woman. And they shall not escape" (I Thessalonians 5:1-3 NKJV).

This of course is a message to ALERT all unbelievers:

The coming of Christ will come as a surprise to the world – *like a thief in the night.* However, this is not true of believers!

Paul continues in verse 4 with these very significant words:

"But you, brethren, are not in darkness, so that this day should overtake you as a thief. You are all sons of light, and the sons of the day. We are not of the night, nor of darkness. Therefore, let us not sleep, as others do, but let us watch and be sober" (I Thessalonians 5:4-6 NKJV).

The teaching is clear. While we cannot know the day or the hour; we are to look for the prophetic signs of His return. When certain signs appear, then we are admonished to know that the day is near. We believe that we are living in the closing days of this dispensation of grace and that the next climatic event is the return of Christ in the air for His Church. We must heed Christ's words when He said,

"Now when these things begin to happen, then look up, and lift up your heads; for your redemption draws near" (Luke 21:28 NKJV).

Many misinterpret the Scripture and declare that it is wrong to be deeply interested in prophecy, yet nearly a third of the Bible is concerned with prophecy. It is wrong to set exact dates – but it is equally wrong to ignore the indications of the nearness of His return.

As His disciples were with Him on the Mount of Olives, He told them of His coming back again to fulfill all prophecy. The disciples then asked the question: "Tell us, *when* ……. and *what?* (Matthew 24:3 NKJV).

As it was

Study the record of the days *before the flood,* says Jesus, if you want an answer to your questions, "when these things shall be" and "what shall be the sign of My coming?" When the conditions before the flood are repeated, then you may know that it is near – yes at the very door. The many conditions are described in three chapters of Genesis as listed below:

1. The social and economic conditions of the world in the days of Noah before the flood (Genesis 4).
2. The dispensational picture of the world in the days of Noah before the flood (Genesis 5).
3. The details of the moral conditions of the world in the days of Noah before the flood (Genesis 6)

So, shall it be

The three chapters deal with three aspects of society in the days before the flood. In the fourth chapter which records the murder of Abel by his brother Cain – we find the first mention of eight characteristics which describe those days:

1. Religious apostasy
2. Travel
3. City building
4. Polygamy
5. Agriculture
6. Music
7. Metallurgy
8. Disrespect for authority

Keep these eight characteristics in mind and notice how *they are being repeated before our very eyes* – and all of them are recorded in Genesis chapter 4, the very days to which Jesus referred when He said:

"But as the days of Noah were, so also will the coming of the Son of man be" (Matthew 24:37 NKJV).

As it was then, so it is today; there are only two religions and their differences are becoming more obvious with each passing day. Man has classified religions into many group-variations and he call them sects, churches, or denominations, etc. However, all of them emerged by God's mercy from the originals:

- False religion based on works.
- True religion based on grace through faith in the death burial and resurrection of Jesus Christ.

By Faith

Genesis does not explain how the practice of sacrificial worship began. Therefore, much speculation is presented in each generation as to why God refused Cain and his offering, but accepted Abel and his offerings in spite of the insight from Hebrews 11:4 wherein we are told that it was "by faith" that Abel offered *to God* a more excellent sacrifice than Cain, through which he obtained witness that *he was righteous,* God testifying of his *gifts;* and through it he being dead *still speaks* (see Hebrews 11:4 NKJV). Abel was moved by faith. Faith comes by hearing, and hearing by the Word of God (Romans 10:17 NKJV).

Our worship spanning from before the flood until the present hour can be grouped under one of these two roots only:

1. The religion of Abel – righteousness based on grace through faith. Wherever the gospel of the grace of God is preached by faith, the Biblical truth is revealed by the Holy Spirit to human beings. Jesus Christ the Son of God preached as Savior and Lord through faith in His blood for the remission of sin – is being ignored or rejected by men and women but acknowledged by God as the true religion of Abel. The seed of redemption promised in Genesis 3:15 seemed to be in jeopardy with the death of Abel, however, God gave Adam and Eve another godly son, Seth (see Genesis 4:26 NKJV), through whom the seed of redemption would be passed all the way to Jesus Christ (see Luke 3:38 NKJV). Praise God!

2. The religion of Cain – is the reverse of Abel's religion and based on self or works-righteousness. Wherever the blood of Jesus Christ is denied, the inspiration of the Bible is rejected, and the dignity of the human person instead of his or her depravity being preached – there you find the false pseudo religion of Cain (see Genesis 4).

Nothing but the Blood of Jesus

It's all in the blood. Wherever the blood of Christ is preached, and received by faith, there is the offering of Abel and where this is not the case it is Cain's religion – probably very impressive but totally worthless. And please don't be deceived, these two are at opposite ends of the spectrum. For the true there can be nothing but the blood of Jesus. We must never forget, and God Himself cannot forget, that all our sins are paid for with the precious blood of Jesus. Remember the promise:

"Knowing that you were not redeemed with corruptible things, like silver or gold, from your aimless conduct received by traditions from your fathers, but with the precious blood of Christ, as a Lamb without blemish and without spot" (1 Peter 1:18-19 NKJV).

Likewise, in true Christianity today there can be:

- No compromise.
- No cooperation.
- No mixing of the two.

Pseudo-Religious Christianity [Cain's religion]

What happened to the church that Jesus Christ built on His death, burial, resurrection and High Priestly ministry? He is the *only* Head of the Church? Can you find it today? Millions of people profess Christianity and claim to be members of His Church – but the Christianity practiced in many local churches today is the Cain version. Cain's religion is a rationally approached pseudo-religious Christianity, void of the blood of Jesus (see Hebrews 9:22). Like Cain himself this version allows many non-biblical entities at the exclusion of God, and the things of God. For example, Amazon lists a Queen Jane's Bible among Christian book sales.

Cain followers have very successfully legalized many non-spiritual institutional customs, traditions and programs:

- These initiatives have estranged many local churches and completely divorced others from the Holy Spirit and His gifts and ministries.
- And they have replaced Him with a rational, philosophical, socially and culturally-oriented pseudo-religious substitute hailed by the world as acceptable because it is worldly, extremely progressive, or the extremely conservative version and politically correct – all at the expense of not being biblically correct.

Only the Word of God can provide the correct answer to our lead-out question. What happened to Jesus Christ's Church built upon His finished work on Calvary – His death, burial, resurrection, ascension and on-going High Priestly ministry from heaven?

He is the only Head of the body, the Church of the Living God, which has the continuing mission of being obedient and useful to Christ's Great Commandment and Great Commission – both corporately and individually. For His glory!

The Restored Church

To hear many tell it including some discouraged church leaders, the church is done for, gone, ineffective and no longer relevant, on and on they go. Their entire assessment is based upon assumptions made through human sensory perception [the five senses, science and reason]. Christ is building a Spiritual Church wherein only Spiritual people "born of the Spirit from above" can belong – yes, in spite of COVID-19.

The early apostolic church placed the highest priority on people having an authentic repentance and personal relationship with Jesus Christ – and "God added to the church such as would be saved."

The Christians' secret, [change]

The restored apostolic church today has the same priority as that found in the Gospels the Book of Acts and the Letters, however knowing the hearts of the religious leaders, Christ, as the Head of the Church, laid the ground work for His ministry while on the earth; which continues in the actions carried on *through* His Spirit-filled disciples bent on being the true Church of Jesus Christ.

Here we are just two decades into the twenty-first century and we find the Traditional and the Institutional American Churches in decline, while the number of unchurched people along with some cults and pseudo-Christian churches, are growing at an alarming fast pace. However, there is a renewed church, a "new wineskin" emerging on the shoulders of the old church.

One of the major reasons for the decline is that old familiar "resistance to change," the traditional and Institutional churches are among the only institutions from the past century that you can visit and find the people locked into what seems to be a time lapse [the church remains just as it was then]. The major change is the sharp decline in membership and attendance due to their rejection of what the Spirit is saying to the churches.

Many people in our churches do not realize that the modern times have ended, and no longer exist. As a result, we have people in the pew sharing two different worldviews. Modernism was the predominant worldview. Today we live in a new multicultural society where tech-savvy postmodernism is the prominent worldview with the smart-phones, social media and other devices. Many of the traditional institutional churches have their doors open with a big "welcome" sign but few takers.

Several other problems traditional churches are coping with:

1. Many people don't attend church because they think differently than did people in the typical modern church of the past sixty or seventy years. Most people of that era placed their faith in science and education. The question of the typical unchurched unbeliever was, "Does God exist?"

2. Today's person lives in a multicultural world where the news media can transport him or her to any place in the world with a simple click of the remote control. Most people have their own computer and internet access which can expose them to many non-Christian beliefs. The question of the young unchurched is, "Which God is real?"

3. Another reason people no longer attend church is that their faith is neither tied to the church nor its leadership. Gallup research discovered that an overwhelming number of church attenders along with the unchurched believed that people "should arrive at their own religious beliefs independent of any church."

Faith no longer tied to the church

The tendency of the older builder generation was to trust the clergy until they gave them some reason not to, which happened in the late 1980's and 1990's when many clergy confessed to relapses in morals and other problems.

Among the younger generations in general, and the Busters in particular; there is the tendency to, not start out trusting the clergy. So, clergy-persons must earn their trust. This does not mean that these people are angry at the institution of the church. When asked why they no longer attend church:

- Many unchurched felt that it really was not that important.
- While 44% said they were too busy. Many others are looking elsewhere for answers to their questions concerning spiritual

matters because they believe the church is answering questions that most of them are not asking.

- When it comes to church attendance, Americans are individualists who pride themselves in their personal autonomy and can do as they please. Individulism could be considered the next new religion on the block in this country.
- Where does the authority lie? Many Americans are convinced that "religious authority" lies with the individual believer and not the church nor the Bible.
- Another factor as in my case was prior exposure to church. We the builder generation and the boomer generation grew up with some exposure to the church. The general expectation of the builders and their parents was they went to church every Sunday morning.
- Many of the boomer generation attended church when they were young because their builder parents took them. Yet many walked away once they graduated from high school or college.
- In contrast, many young adults today have rarely attended a church or not at all. They question, why should I attend church when there are so many other things to do?

It's imperative that today's church leadership give good answers to the younger generation's questions. "We have always done it that way" is not the appropriate answer. Churches are going to be countered by:

- Beaches and other recreations are open around the clock.
- People think Sunday morning is no longer sacred.
- Many rivals have come to the front to compete with the church for the hearts and souls of the people on Sunday.
- With the repeal of the blue laws, merchants can be opened on Sunday as well as the other six days,
- Many people have chosen to work on Sundays.
- Many chose to sleep-in.

Two things that hinder

The Bible clearly speaks of two things that hinder the Holy Spirit and the Word from being effective in accomplishing their purpose:

1. religious tradition
2. unbelief

Reigious Tradition

This present age will be one of storms for the church. In Matthew 14, we see that the disciples were in the storm not because they disobeyed Christ (as Jonah did), but because they obeyed Him. If we obey the Spirit and the Word of God, there will be suffering and persecution, but Christ, our High Priest is praying for us and will soon come and take us home. *The secret is faith.* Unbelief and fear always go together, just as faith and peace always go together. As Christians, I pray we will not be of "little faith."

In Matthew 15 we see Christ withdrawing from open confrontation with the Scribes and Pharisees as He teaches His disciples and prepares them for His death on the cross. However, in (vv. 1-2 NKJV) these religious leaders were as always looking for some charge to bring against Jesus. They accused His disciples of violating the traditions of the Jewish elders by not going through the ceremonial washings when they ate. It is important to note that the Pharisees honored their traditions above the written Word of God. "It is a greater offense to teach anything contrary to the voice of the Rabbis, than to contradict Scripture itself," says the *Mishna* [a collection of Jewish traditions]. Rabbi Eleazer said, "He who expounds the Scriptures in opposition to the tradition has no share in the world to come." Christ condemns their washings (see Matthew 23:25-26 NKJV).

Notice how Christ always silences His accusers using the Word of God. He points out their own disobedience to Exodus 20:12 and 21:17. By dedicating their possessions to God, the Pharisees released themselves from any obligation to care for their parents.

How many "religious" people there are even today who carefully keep traditions, yet openly disobey the Word of God!

The nature of their sin is identified in (vv. 4-6) as dishonoring parents in a cleverly devised way. Some claimed they could not financially assist their parents because they had dedicated a certain sum of money to God, who was greater than their parents. The Rabbis granted this exception to the commandments of Moses and thus in effect nullified God's law (see v. 6).

Therefore, the Lord said; "Inasmuch as these people draw near with their mouths and honor Me with their lips, but have removed their hearts far from Me, and their fear toward Me is taught by the commandment of men."

Christ quoted this passage, Isaiah 29:13, to show that their religion was not of the heart but was merely outward show. We must constantly remind ourselves that truth comes from the heart [you must be "born again – from above"]:

- We love from the heart (Romans 10:9-10)
- We love from the heart (Matthew 22:37)
- We sing from the heart (Colossians 3:16)
- We obey from the heart (Romans 6:17)
- We give from the heart (2 Corinthians 9:7)
- We pray from the heart (Psalm 51:10, 17)

Contrast between God's truth and traditions of humankind

Human traditions	**God's Truth**
Outward forms for Outward show	Inward faith brings liberty
Burdensome rules, the Letter of the law	Basic biblical principles, the spirit of the Law
Man-made laws that exalt men	God-breathed words that humbles a person

People could defile themselves *ceremonially* under the Old Covenant by eating something unclean – but they would defile themselves *morally* by saying something sinful (see James 3:5 NKJV).

Ceremonial defilement can be dealt with through ceremonial means – but moral defilement corrupts a person's soul.

Here Jesus clearly distinguished between the ceremonial requirements of the law and its inviolable moral standard. Ceremonial defilement could be dealt with through ceremonial means.

Moral defilement

Moral defilement corrupts a person's soul. The Christians at Corinth had a fellow church member who lived in moral sin. So, Paul commanded them:

"In the name of our Lord Jesus Christ, when you are gathered together along with my spirit, with the power of our Lord Jesus Christ, deliver such a one to Satan for the destruction of the flesh, that his spirit may be saved in the day of the Lord Jesus" (I Corinthians 5:4, 5 NKJV).

This passage refers to God turning the adulterer over to Satan for physical affliction or even physical death. After being separated from the spiritual protection of the church, the ideal is the offender would recognize his sin, repent, and return to the church.

Herein is another blessed truth given. This man living in terrible sin was a child of God. But he was to be left to punishment *"for the destruction of the flesh"* in order that *"the spirit may be saved in the day of the Lord Jesus."* God cannot punish His saints in hell – therefore the Christian's chastening must come now, in this life. In I Corinthians 11, Paul addresses the church at Corinth which had divisions, quarrels, worldliness, a flippant observance of the Lord's Supper, without any judging of sin in their lives. Paul wrote,

"But let a man examine himself, and so let him eat of the bread and drink of the cup. For he who drinks in an unworthy manner eats and drinks judgment to himself, not discerning the Lord's body.

For this reason, many are weak and sick among you, and many sleep. For if we would judge ourselves, we would not be judged. But when we are judged, we are chastened by the Lord, that we may not be condemned with the world" (vv. 28-32 NKJV).

All church discipline has restoration as its goal. The condition of the church at Corinth fit many local churches in America today. In the Great

Commission, Jesus commanded that we *"teach all that He commanded."* This is the reason why we must be born again from above; and receive new hearts. Otherwise we would be unsaved, and this is not pertinent to the unsaved.

Unbelief

Having looked at religious traditions; we will now look at the second hindrance which is moving from belief in God to – *unbelief.* Just because you have faith, it doesn't automatically produce victory in your life. As I said in an earlier section, your unbelief will counterbalance and short-circuit your faith – until you get rid of the unbelief. Often the problem is not a lack of faith, but rather too much unbelief.

In Matthew 17:18-20 NKJV, the disciples were not able to cast out a demon from a young epileptic son. The father appealed to Jesus for help. The Bible says, *"Jesus rebuked the demon, and it came out of him; and the child was cured from that very hour.* When the disciples asked, *"Why could we not cast it out?"*

Jesus said to them, *"Because of your unbelief."* Much of the body of Christ excuses this by:

- Well, we are just people.
- We ask if it doesn't happen, it's because of God's sovereign will.
- Those things passed away with the apostles.

The church is supposed to have the answers for the world – but apparently, we aren't using what we do have. Christ's response to the disciples is the same for the church today. People should be able to come to the church for salvation, healing, deliverance, and blessing [emotional and financial]. However, many local churches corporately and individually:

- Send their sick to a human doctor.
- Send the poor and destitute to the local government or some other social agency for assistance.
- Send the mental and emotionally disturbed to the psychiatrist.

The local churches have come up with many different doctrinal statements to justify its powerlessness and ineffectiveness. Certainly, this should not be! God's answers and solutions are in the Word of God for all the Church.

Sources of unbelief

Normally our unbelief comes from one or more of the following sources:

1. Ignorance – I don't know because I've never learned it.
2. Wrong teaching – I don't believe in miracles because I was taught that miracles ended when the last apostle died.
3. Natural thinking – it's God's will that I be sick because I prayed, but when I went to the doctor, he said I was getting worse!

I believe all sin and defilement begins with unbelief (see John 16:9). Many Christians open themselves up for unbelief; because they do not have the Word of God in them (see John 5:38). Unbelief feeds on what we read or hear especially on the newscasts, college campuses, workplaces, across social media, and the societal and cultural opinions of others.

Go on to perfection

In Hebrews 6, these Hebrew Christians had become dissatisfied because they had nothing they could see, handle, touch as they had in Judaism. The joyous state which had characterized these believers in the early days of their hearing the Gospel had not been a continuing experience.

- They had known in their hearts the glow of God's grace that only the first love of a believer can experience.
- They had heard the glorious Gospel of the grace of God, their affections had been set upon Him who is seated at the right hand of the Majesty on high.
- They had exercised faith in His finished work, and they had realized that their Savior and keeper was in heaven.

But true faith must be tried and unless it is maintained, "hope deferred makes the heart sick" (Proverbs 13:12 NKJV).

The writer exhorts them, "Cast not away therefore your confidence which hath great recompense of reward. For you have need of patience, that, after you have done the will of God, you might receive the promise" (Hebrews 10:35-36).

From chapter 3 verse 1 we know that the "holy brethren" had already acknowledged the coming of the Lamb and had left the first things of Christianity. He urged them not to return to these things which they had already accepted and experienced but to go on to greater things, [perfection] which points to the full revelation which God the Father had made concerning Himself in the Person of His only begotten Son, the Lord Jesus Christ (see II Corinthians 4:6; 5:19).

The Son, crucified, buried, risen, ascended and glorified and now sits at the right hand of the Majesty on the throne of grace and glory – and all believers are to set their affections on Him (see Colossians 3:1-3).

- We are to go on to perfection of knowledge, spiritually speaking – knowledge imparted by the Holly Spirit.
- We are to go on to perfection in the knowledge of the mysteries and doctrine of the Gospel of the grace of God.
- They were to leave the earthly system of Judaism for Christ.

The elementary principles of Christ

The early church went into the Dark Ages of the church as men became more interested in doctrine than experience. We must remember that the first church, the Body of Christ, was birthed not in doctrine only, but on the streets of Jerusalem in supernatural experiences, accompanied by physical and emotional signs and wonders that caused others looking on to think they were drunk. Denominationalism established during the last 500 years of church restoration has lost its life to networking. For us to go on to perfection [maturity] means to turn away from all things that would draw our attention from Christ and things eternal and cause us to look back to the less-fortunate elements of the world. Hebrews 6:1-2 NKJV constitute a six-statement explanation of what the apostle meant by "*having left the beginning of the word of Christ and going on to maturity:*

1. Repentance from dead works – and deliverance from the traditions of the elders that made the "Word of God of no effect" (see Mark 7:13 NKJV).
2. Faith toward God – was the second doctrine of Christ to be reestablished by members as they have *faith.*

3. <u>Baptisms</u> – this was the restoration of the great commission in the name of the Father, and the Son, and the Holy Spirit. Now emphasis of the manifestation of the graces and gifts of the Holy Spirit (see 1 Corinthians 12:7-11 NKJV).

4. <u>Laying on of hands</u> – the experiential truth of "divine healing" was restored. Oral Roberts was one of the best-known American healing ministers.

5. <u>Resurrection of the dead</u> – refers to the resurrection of all people at the end times (see Revelation 20:11-15). The resurrection is an Old Testament teaching (see Isaiah 26:19; Daniel 12:2 NKJV) which was taught in first-century Judaism, especially by the Pharisees. To Christians, belief in the bodily resurrection of Jesus was essential, for *without* His resurrection there is no forgiveness of sin (see 1 Corinthians 15:12-17 NKJV).

New understanding of such Scriptures as those recorded below will come to the church:

I am the living bread which came down from heaven. If anyone eats of this bread, he will live forever ...... This is the bread which came down from heaven – not as your fathers ate the manna and are dead. He who eats this bread will live forever (John 6:51, 58).

Jesus Christ, who has abolished death, and has brought life and immortality to light through the gospel (2 Timothy 1:10 NKJV).

*The law of the spirit of life in Christ Jesus has made me free from the law of sin and death (*Romans 8:2 NKJV).

6. <u>Eternal Judgment</u> – refers to the doctrine that everyone will be judged by the Great Judge, Jesus Christ, the Scriptures note two judgements:

One judgment for believers, in which Jesus determines every believer's reward (see 1 Corinthians 15:12-17 NKJV).

The other a judgment of condemnation on unbelievers (see Revelation 20:11-15 NKJV).

Each restoration truth of the Holy Spirit has enabled the church to appropriate more of the full redemptive work of Christ. The Holy Spirit has been commissioned by Jesus Christ to lead the church into *all truth*. Fullness of truth will bring fulness of life. When the church reaches full maturity in Christ it will come into all that Christ presently is: *"As He is, so are we in this world"* (1 John 4:17 NKJV).

The priesthood of *all* believers

The Christian Church is the sum total of all who believe that Jesus Christ is our Savior and Lord. As stated throughout this book, the church has been commissioned by Christ Himself, to carry His message down through the ages to constantly *changing* cultures. The 21st century, like those centuries gone before has seen within the first two decades, the accelerated expansion and changing of civilization at a phenomenal rate. This gives the present generation the grave task of continuous restoration with the Christian Church.

Therefore, the church will continue to face new problems in the field of Christian doctrine and ethics. Pastors and other church leaders realize that the church must always be in the process of self-renewal through the dynamic power of the gospel – if it is to be relevant in the postmodern world to which it has been sent by our Lord.

Recovery of a biblical basis

A significant fact in much of the American Church today among Christians are those who are spiritually alive to the life-changing challenges of the Gospel and not satisfied just being mere pew-sitters. The Book of Acts is the best documentation of the priesthood of all believers and the chief source for its restoration today:

- Paul uses many metaphors in his description of all believers as "members of the family of God," as part of a *"growing"* temple of God (Ephesians 2:18-22 NKJV).
- The Holy Spirit has bestowed on *each* Christian a spiritual gift or gifts for the *unity* of the whole body. Paul used the human body as an analogy (1 Corinthians 12:12-27 NKJV) to expand on this whole "body" concept.

- While stressing the diversity of gifts, (vv. 4-11 NKJV), Paul also stressed the single *source* of the spiritual gifts being the Holy Spirit.
- We also learn from these passages that the gifts are not something to seek, but to be *"received"* from the Spirit "as He will." It is He alone who "works" or energizes (v. 6) all gifts as He chooses.

Paul counseled the early Christians and us, "to present *yourselves* as a *living sacrifice* to God, dedicated to His service and pleasing to Him" (see Romans 12:1 NKJV). The Scriptures use many names, metaphors, and parables to describe the church and its members. As stated earlier, throughout this work there are many references to the *functions* of [all] the members of Christ's body. To God be the glory. Amen

QUESTIONS FOR DISCUSSION & REFLECTION: CHAPTER 8

1. How did Jesus say the people of the world will be when He returns?
2. Discuss the dangers of date-setting about Jesus' return.
3. Discuss prophetic biblical signs of Christ's return, happening in this present age?
4. Specifically, to whom are the warnings of 1 Thessalonians 5:1-3 directed?
5. Contrast the two kinds of religion in the present world with Cain's religion and Abel's faith.

SECTION THREE

FORWARD
IN FAITH

CHAPTER NINE

FOR HIS GLORY

Now these things became our examples, to the intent that we should not lust after evil things, as they also lusted. And do not become idolaters as were some of them. As it is written, "The people sat down to eat and drink, and rose up to play." Nor let us commit sexual immorality, as some of them did, and in one day twenty-three thousand fell; nor let us tempt Christ, as some of them also tempted, and were destroyed by serpents; nor complain, as some of them also complained and were destroyed by the destroyer. Now all these things happened to them as examples, and they were written for our admonition, upon whom the ends of the ages have come (1 Corinthians 10:6-11 NKJV).

Often writing under the inspiration of the Holy Spirit, Paul called the entire Old Testament comprised of both the Law and the prophets, by one word, the Law (see 1 Corinthians 14:21, 34; Genesis 3:16 NKJV). We realize that the natural commandments and ordinances of the Law produce *bondage;* while the spirit of the Law brings *liberty.*

However, many of the natural concepts of the Law are not commandments, but rather spiritual principles or *examples to live by.* In addition, some examples of God's severe judgments upon sin are displayed also.

Some in the church at Corinth had fallen into dire error and immorality, note the Scripture text above, Paul used Israel's disobedience to show the Corinthian converts God's displeasure with them – and the ultimate consequences of their own sin. Therefore, we can readily see that the Spirit revealed by the Law many *examples* of right and wrong attitudes, motives, and actions *to judge our lives by* (see 1 Corinthians 2:9-10 NKJV). Emphasis added throughout.

Old Testament Examples

A very positive example is Daniel. Many Christians do not understand the necessity of fasting and confessing their forefathers' sins to free themselves of the spiritual bondage of inherited generational sins. Daniel's prayer and confession are spiritual examples for us to live by. The Scripture said, "Daniel had an excellent spirit" (study very prayerfully and carefully Daniel 9:3-19).

- He prayed despite an ordinance passed against it (see Daniel 6:7-10 NKJV).
- The Bible does not record any sin that Daniel committed – but we are all humbled I'm sure by his humility in praying as he did, *"We have sinned!"*

David

When David committed adultery with Bathsheba and had her husband killed, God took immediate action. He dispatched Nathan to David with a message wrapped in a parable. David immediately judged the man in the parable and in doing so; he announced sentence on himself (see Matthew 12:37 NKJV).

David repented of his sin and God immediately forgave him – however, God told him that the sword would never leave his house (see 2 Samuel 12:10-13). An important note here, although God had mercy and gracefully forgave David – David still *reaped what he sowed*. This example points out to us very vividly and gives assurance of both God's mercy and His righteous judgments.

We see here, that even repentance doesn't change one word of God's eternal law [truth], *"Do not be deceived, God is not mocked; for whatsoever a man sows, that he will also reap"* (Galatians 6:7 NKJV). Emphasis added throughout.

New Testament Examples

The *principle* of "sowing and reaping" was well-known to everyone in the largely agricultural society [sow corn seeds – you'll receive a corn harvest]. Otherwise "the sowing" is a vain attempt to "mock" God; and for *any* church or Christian to think that if he or she sows to their *flesh* – they will escape the harvest of judgment and destruction that comes upon those who participate in sin is very much mistaken! In Hebrews 12:4-8 NKJV, God makes a plain statement:

"Ye have not resisted unto blood, striving against sin. And ye have forgotten the exhortation which speaketh unto you as unto children, My son, despise not thou the chastening of the Lord, nor faint when thou art rebuked of him: for whom the Lord loveth He chasteneth, and scourgeth every son whom he receiveth. If ye endure chastening, God dealeth with you as with sons; for what son is he whom the father chasteneth not? But if ye be without chastisement, whereof all are partakers, then are ye bastards, and not sons. KJV

Again, God states plainly, that every child of God is chastened:

- One who does not have chastisement from God is a bastard and not a son (v. 8).
- We are told plainly in (v. 4) that chastisement comes because of sin, "Ye have not resisted unto blood, striving against sin.
- Later in the passage we are told that God chastens us that *"we might be partakers of His holiness"* (v. 10).
- God's chastisement purges us from our sins and makes us fit for heaven and His presence.

But since every Christian receives chastisement, then every Christian commits sin.

In his writings Paul often used the Greek word *"sarx"* to denote the "flesh" meaning "the entire fallen being, including, *spirit, soul, and body,* is affected by sin. The Scriptures make it clear, either we are walking in the Spirit or we are walking in the flesh. We will secure the victory if we are obedient to the passage, "Walk in the Spirit and you shall not fulfill the lusts of the flesh" (Galatians 5:16-17 NKJV).

In Galatians 5:16-23 Paul contrasts the works of the two different walks. Walking in the flesh he lists seventeen works of the flesh:

- Adultery – sexual relations outside of marriage (see Galatians 5:19; Matthew 5:32; 15:19 also see Hosea 8:7).
- Fornication – all other manner of unlawful sexual relations (Matthew 5:32).
- Uncleanness – all forms of sexual perversion (v. 16; Romans 1:21-32; 6:19).
- Lasciviousness – anything tending to promote sexual sin (v. 19; 2 Peter 2:17).
- Idolatry – passionate affections upon things (v. 20; Colossians 3:5).
- Witchcraft – the practice of dealing with evil spirits (v. 20; Revelation 22:15).
- Hatred – bitter dislike; abhorrence (v. 20; Ephesians 2:15-16).
- Variance – discord, dissensions, quarreling (v. 20; Romans 1:29).
- Emulations – envies, jealousies, outdo others, zeal (v. 20; Romans 10:2).
- Wrath – indignation, fierceness (v. 20; Ephesians 4:31; Colossians 3:8).
- Strife – contentions, payback (v. 20; 1 Corinthians 12:20).
- Seditions – disorder, parties, divisions (v. 20; 1 Corinthians 3:3).
- Heresies – goes astray from truth (v. 20; Acts 5:17; Galatians 2).
- Envying – jealous of others' blessings (v. 21; Matthew 27:18).
- Murders – to kill; hatred (v. 21; 1 John 3:15).
- Drunkenness – living intoxicated (v. 21; Romans 13:13).
- Reveling – rioting, sinful activities (v. 21; 1 Peter 4:3; Romans 13:13).

The Spirit through Paul ends with dire warning, *"Those who practice such things shall not inherit the kingdom of God"* (v. 21). Don't be deceived! The Scriptures distinctly concludes that the only way to overcome these fleshly desires is to live in the power of the Holy Spirit and the Word of God; as He works through our spirit (see Galatians 5:25). As we walk in the Spirit, He develops and displays the nine-fold fruit of the Spirit [Christ's character] in us:

- Love – humility, esteem, devotion, mutuality (v. 22; 1 Corinthians 13; Romans 8:28).
- Joy – rejoice even among the worse circumstances (v. 22; Philippians 4:11).
- Peace – keep hearts and minds, no anxiety (v22; Philippians 4:7).
- Longsuffering – power under control (v. 22; II Corinthians 6:3-10).
- Kindness – goodness, patience (v. 22: 1 Corinthians 13:4).
- Goodness – righteousness (v. 22; Romans 15:14; II Thessalonians 1:11).
- Faithfulness – faithful, faith (Galatians 5:22; 3:10).
- Gentleness – meekness, submissive, teachable spirit (v. 22; II Corinthians 10:1).
- Self-control – flesh, body under submission, temperance, self-mastery (1 Corinthians 7:9; 10:23, 31).

I pray that through reading and studying this section on the Christian's walk, you will become fully aware of the benefits of the Holy Spirit, resident in you sanctifying you from the inside out; as He develops and displays the fruit of the Spirit within you for all to see.

Spiritually-minded

Paul warned that without the fruit of the Spirit no person can enter the kingdom of God. Living without these Christian character traits does not in any way glorify God in the world. In an earlier chapter we discussed the fact that there are only two kinds of religion, "right" and "wrong." Of course, the person with the "right religion" is walking in the Spirit and righteousness automatically displaying these traits:

- This "righteousness" *"imputed"* then means [justification – put to our account] through the "blood of Jesus," giving us right standing before GOD.
- This "righteousness" *"imparted"* then means [sanctification – made a part of life] and gives right standing before MEN through the "cross of Christ." So, they believe we are Christians – the "fruit of the Spirit is imparted by the Spirit.

Both are a part of salvation (see James 2:14-26). Sin is charged to Christ's account not ours – and that based purely on grace (see 2 Corinthians 5:21; Philippians 18). Isn't salvation wonderful?

Carnally-minded

Instead of being spiritually-minded many Christians are carnally-minded and finding themselves weak and being conformed or shaped by society's secular worldview. This happens when Christians fail to obediently seek the divinely revealed truth of God's Word (see II Peter 1:1-3; 1 Peter 1:18-21). The Scripture warns us, "God's people perish from a lack of knowledge." Thus, many carnal Christians are still on the milk of the Word; when they should by now be further along and eating solid food and teaching others.

Sadly, people in this state many times are deceived into thinking they are people of great authority with God, because of their position in church or workplace and they may by position bear a certain amount of authority, but without the knowledge of the truth of God's Word, they are powerless. They live closer to the world in their worldview and lifestyle than toward God and His Word. This is the expected end for any Christian who fails to seek God's face in prayer, study and obediently apply the revealed truths of God's Word in *every* detail of their daily life.

Your love for God and others, repentance, forgiveness, obedience, and a [biblically] renewed mind promote a healthy spiritual life.

Living in the Spirit

It bears repeating, Paul stressed that carnality is countered by living in the Spirit and the Word of God. There is no condemnation because we are *equipped* and *empowered* by the Spirit of God to live for Christ (Romans 8:1).

There were tremendous differences in the ministry of the disciples before and after the power of the Spirit and the Word of God working in tandem developed and clothed them – the same holds true for the *true* believer today:

- Jesus had told them that as His disciples; the Holy Spirit was already with them (see John 14:17).
- If any one does not have the Holy Spirit, he or she does not belong to Christ (see Romans 8:9).
- The Spirit of God makes His abode in every person who trusts in Jesus Christ (1 Corinthians 6:19, 20; 12:13).
- When there is no evidence of the Spirit's presence by the fruit of the Spirit He produces (carefully study Galatians 5:22, 23), a person has no legitimate claim to Christ as Savior and Lord.

Why our revivals fail

The Spirit must penetrate and possess all our being. He must control us in all His lordship. God will not violate your will, nor does He manipulate you.

The divine empowerment of the Holy Spirit is of God in and through you, but enablement always depends on your total obedience and corporation.

Paul is a good example for all ministers of the gospel; he knew that God's power must so *saturate* his message so that the *faith* of the converts would rest upon the Spirit's power:

"And my speech and my preaching were not with persuasive words of human wisdom, but with a demonstration of the Spirit and power, so that your faith might not rest on men's wisdom, but on God's power, that your faith should not be in the wisdom of men but in the power of God" (1 Corinthians 2:4-5 NKJV).

Many local Christian churches in this country glory like the Corinthians:

- in their own strength,
- in their wealth,
- in their gifts.

Christ was glorified in His humility and death. Isn't it ironic that the Church at Corinth was so gifted, and yet so weak; especially during a time when history reports that the preaching of the cross was so dominant in the early church (1 Corinthians 1:18)?

Paul, a New Testament example

Though Paul had his strengths (see Philippians 3:4-9), he wanted to *model* Christ's humility by presenting his "weaknesses." Then the "strength of the gospel message" could be clearly seen. Paul's ways should still be our ways. Our contemporary methods in no way work as well as his old-time ways worked. He turned the Gentile world upside down.

Far too often *our methods* conform to the world [society] rather than transform the world. The proof is in the pudding! We should study the Scriptures to discover Paul's and the other apostles' old-time ways; so that we can experience similar results:

- The early chapters of the Book of Acts give many examples for proper church organization and growth (1 Corinthians 4:17).
- Paul said that even his sufferings were examples for us to follow (see 1 Timothy 1:16).
- Paul's integrity in handling finances was impeccable (see 2 Corinthians 8:19-21; Acts 20:31-35).
- Christ also suffered for us – leaving us His example (see 2 Peter 2:21).
- Of course, the greatest of all examples is Jesus Christ. Imitate Him!

The New Testament believer's authority

The apostles were given great authority to conduct Christ's business (see Acts 8:14; 11:22; 15:27; 17:15). Listen to the apostle to the Gentiles:

"Now concerning our brother Apollos, I strongly urged him to come to you with the brethren, but he was quite unwilling to come at this time; however, he will come when he has a convenient time" (1 Corinthians 16:12 NKJV).

It's obvious that Paul *did not* try exercising control over Apollo's ministry. Although Apollos refused his request, Paul didn't accuse him of rebellion; he respected his convictions. The Scriptures record that Paul was the apostle to the Gentiles; nevertheless, he didn't judge another man's (Christ's) servant as a rebel when he didn't submit to his desires (see Romans 11:13; Galatians 2:7-8).

While Christian pastors do have authority, it is very different from worldly authority. I was a leader with much authority for more than twenty-six years in the U.S. Army [retired in 1984], and after that, more than thirty years in Church leadership as a pastor, teacher, and author. The leaders' authority and its usage in both vocations are very different:

1. Christians are never to seek to bend others to their will but bring them to respond to Jesus Christ.
2. The Christian rejects power and position as a basis for authority.
3. Unlike secular or worldly authority this kind of authority rests purely on a supernatural basis. Its only because Jesus Himself lives by His Spirit, resident in each believer and corporate community and will act to vindicate the authority of His Spirit-filled servants without their action.

Like Paul, as present-day New Testament believer-priests we also wield great authority:

- Paul said that we are ambassadors for Christ (see 2 Corinthians 5:20).
- Peter said we are a holy priesthood (see 1 Peter 2:4) and a royal priesthood, a new people (see 1 Peter 2:9).

The sole claim to any authority the Christian has is that Jesus speaks to the people by His Spirit through him or her by both their lifestyle [incarnating the Word] and His teaching [communicating the Word].

A new people

The Bible primarily teaches that Christ died for a people, not a person. I am not discounting the individual act of repentance and faith that comes in response to hearing and believing the gospel. The Holy Spirit saves you personally, but the Scriptures focus on the salvation and creation of a new people. We are a unified group of people who are set apart for God's use. His own special people: God protects those who are His. Jesus said,

"My sheep hear my voice, and they know me." God's people hear the voice of their Shepherd, and they follow, not the man, but Jesus who speaks through them.

In my book *According to Pattern,* I point out that unlike the Old Testament priesthood, in which only those who were born into a certain tribe could be priests – in the New Testament, all who are truly born again [from above] and adopted into God's family are priests and have the privilege and responsibility of offering all their activities as spiritual sacrifices to God.

The New Testament distinguishes the false believers in contrast to His spiritual "new people" by the distortions that appear in their lifestyles and teachings. You cannot separate your Christianity from the new community that you are born into when you believe and receive the gospel. And just like any people group has distinctives, God's new people have things about them that the watching world should immediately notice about the people of God. Just a couple of examples:

- The watching world should be able to easily spot *grace* in the people of God. Peter reminds us that before we had not received mercy, but now we have received mercy. This mercy shown by God gave us salvation – who did not deserve it. Therefore, it stands to reason we would be identified by this kind of grace in our interactions with one another. Since our heritage is grace, so should our practice be marked by grace also. Are you quick to *show love* to people who don't ask for it? The apostle John said this is how the world will recognize Christians (John 13:34-35).
- Christians *give generously* of their resources, time and energy in thanksgiving for all that God has given to us in sending His Son to die for us. We actively look for *ways to be generous,* cultivating a spirit of generosity within ourselves. We look for opportunities to give to one another as they have need.

A 90-year old woman commented: "I have served the Lord so long that I can hardly tell the difference between a blessing and a trial."

Therefore, James admonishes us to, *"Count it all joy"* as we face the various kinds of trials (James 1:2). Paul said, *"We rejoice in hope of the glory of God"* (Romans 5:2).

I think that most Christians overlook the privilege that as a New Testament believer-priest, he or she can go straight to the throne of grace [God's throne] through Jesus Christ to find help in time of need. Praise God!

Give yourself away

I do not encourage sin. I must solemnly tell every Christian who reads this that sin is a fearful thing. It brings unnumbered troubles! Sin has never paid anybody. It is the most hateful thing, the most feared, the most despised in all the universe of God! With all my being I plead with Christians everywhere to flee from sin, judge sin, to search their hearts daily to confess and forsake sin.

Thousands of Christians speak openly of being saved by *grace*, but often they mean grace plus something else. I know preachers who say they believe in salvation by grace, but they believe that one cannot be saved except by:

- Being baptized by immersion only
- Attending service every Sunday
- Paying tithe
- Obeying in every thought, word, and deed
- Working hard for it, "holding out faith"

They have not understood salvation by grace. Neither have they understood the clear Bible teaching of how wicked, how incurable, is the *carnal mind,* self-deceived and deceiving others, so that the poor lost sinner can never deserve salvation to get it – and a saved sinner can never deserve salvation to keep it! Since the old nature (body of sin), and since all Christians sin, whether he or she is conscious of any known sin, he is still deceiving himself if he says that he has no sin (1 John 1:8).

Since every Christian is commanded to pray daily, *"Forgive us our sins"* (see Like 11:4), then we conclude that God Himself must provide a salvation that includes His own perfect righteousness given freely to the undeserving sinner!

Remember, the man who is incapable of saving himself is equally incapable of keeping himself.

- In Romans 12:1, 2, Paul admonishes believers to "present your body a living sacrifice" – meaning they should use their bodies to serve and obey God in all things. Remember the child of God is in the Head, Jesus Christ – not the tail!
- Additionally, Romans 6:13, focuses on the individual parts of the body such as hands or mouth. Believer-priests are not to present the parts of their body as a means for sinning. By just considering our own body; it's very evident that each part is useless without our head. Notice, no part of our human body can converse with any other part without direction from the head. That is the cause of so much division in the local churches today. The parts are trying to exercise "authority" they do not possess. Though the arm may possess tremendous "power," once severed from the body through which the head communicates to it – really has no life – it is useless and ineffective because it has no authority to use that power.

When we chose to use the standard dictionary as our only source for meanings, we can be easily misled. For example, biblically speaking the word "power" has two applications in the Greek:

1. Dunamus – from which we get the resurrection "power" like dynamite [BANG]" (Ephesians 1:21).
2. Exousias – from which we get "authority" which is "delegated [POWER]" (Ephesians 6:12; Colossians 1:13).

Set Apart unto God

Salvation serves sanctification as a foundation serves a building. No matter how beautiful the building is in appearance, it will not be able to stand the storms of life unless built upon a solid foundation. Likewise, no matter how adorned, and beautiful life may be lived, it will not stand in the face of divine tests and the storms of life – unless he or she has been made a new creation in Christ. Why does God save sinners?

- God saves sinners so they might be conformed to the image of His Son.
- He saves us so that we might bring Him praise, honor, and glory not only now, but throughout eternity (Ephesians 1:12, 14).
- We bring glory to Him in this life as we work out our salvation which God calls for (Philippians 2:12).

Often overlooked is the fact that the believer is a new creature in Christ. Just as salvation affects the whole person, so sanctification affects the totality of the person. The new person grows in the grace and knowledge of Christ and becomes more Christlike – as:

- The mind of Christ is being formed in the believer.
- His or her walk will affect other believers.
- They will have and show compassion to all – not just other believers.
- The redemption of God quickens the awareness of the needs of others in the redeemed.
- Christians not only recognize and act upon the needs of humankind for redemption, but also that they may be delivered from bondage resulting from the curse that all humanity suffers because of sin.

Christians should never forget that the work of sanctification requires considering ourselves dead to sin and yielding to Christ's work of sanctification through the Holy Spirit in all areas of our lives. Salvation, justification, and sanctification work in tandem in regeneration. As Christians are transformed into His image. God's reconciling and justifying work outside us in Jesus Christ and His regenerating and progressive sanctifying work to maturity within us by His Spirit through His ministry of teaching (John 16:12-15).

Additionally, praying according to the will of God as directed by the Spirit (Romans 8:26; Ephesians 6:18). The spiritual believer will be exercising in the spiritual gifts given to empower him or her by the Spirit (I Corinthians 12:7). By the power of the Spirit he or she will learn to war victoriously against the flesh (Romans 8:26; Galatians 5:16-17). In summary, the fulness of the Spirit is key to maturity through the process of sanctification in the believer.

QUESTIONS FOR DISCUSSION & REFLECTION: CHAPTER 9

1. Discuss how the natural commandments and ordinances of the Law produce *bondage,* while the spirit of the Law brings *liberty.*
2. Discuss the situation with converts in the Corinthian Church and contrast it with converts today. Are there similarities? Why?
3. Daniel's prayer and confession are spiritual examples for us to live by (see I Corinthians 2:9-10).
4. Contrast walking in the Spirit with walking in the flesh (again study Romans 8:1; John 14:17).
5. Discuss Paul's reaction to Apollo's refusal to come to him when he requested. How did Paul respond? How would you have responded?

CHAPTER TEN

APPROPRIATED BY FAITH

"But you have an anointing from the Holy One and you know all things. I have not written to you because you do not know the truth, but because you know it, and that no lie is of the truth" (1 John 2:20-21).

In Old Testament times prophets, priests, and kings were anointed with oil to set them apart for God's service. The oil symbolized the Holy Spirit coming upon them both to set apart and to divinely equip them for service. The word Christ is the English for the Greek term for the Hebrew "Messiah." Both words mean "anointed one."

God *anointed* Jesus of Nazareth with the Holy Spirit and power. He went about doing well and healing all who were under the devil's power, because God was with Him" (see Acts 10:38). The term *Christian* means follower of Jesus Christ, the Anointed One.

The Scripture assigns the term "anointing" to all who belong to Christ. Every Christian ordained or not can rest assured that Christ wants them to live an anointed life. He that anointed us is God (2 Corinthians 12:1). You have the anointing from the Holy One (1 John 2:20).

But the anointing which you have received from Him abides in you, and you do not need that anyone teach you, but as the same anointing teaches you concerning all things, and is true, and is not a lie, and just as it has taught you, you will abide in Him (1 John 2:27).

Appropriated by faith

The degree to which any Christian receives this anointing and is conscious of doing so depends on the closeness of his or her walk with the Anointed One, and the extent to which, by faith, he or she appropriates it. The anointing is in the Christian from regeneration but may not be very active. In all our Christian experiences, faith is the appropriating means.

Because of God's presence within the early Christians *"a number of people believed and turned to the Lord"* (Acts 11:21). Perhaps the lack of such observable spiritual results today, are due in part to our lack of *God's anointing* upon our lives and ministries.

The Scripture says, *"You have the anointing from the Holy One."* God is attempting to impress upon us the availability of His anointing power to us in all of life. Shamefully many Christians avoid even a conversation concerning the anointing, for fear of being accused of extreme fanatical behavior. I'm sure Satan is pleased with them. Our coolness toward the anointing over the years has produced a people who are very content to live and minister on a mostly *human* level. Very noticeable in our churches today is the difference between:

- A Scripture lesson read *with* or *without* the anointing.
- A solo beautifully sung with merely human skill and quality performance – and a solo sung with the anointing of the Lord on the singer.

Why do some sermons seem so lifeless? Why are so many sermons like a mere secular lecture?

- Undoubtedly the messenger did not receive the message from the Lord.
- Another reason is the messenger truly does not believe the message. Notice the difference between sermons delivered with superficial faith and enthusiasm and – one given when the anointing is upon the minister.

Divine spiritual reality

God desires that we continually receive the experience of His anointing, putting His super on our natural. He wants us to learn to depend upon His added enabling, presence and power. Some may talk in more modern terms, but there is a divine *spiritual* reality which God has for us – without the anointing we would be operating in the flesh.

The more we minister, the more we need our power renewed. The busier you become, the more you need spiritual refreshment and replenishing. It is not just mental and physical exhaustion that you experience. Without a fresh anointing of power, you will become a spiritual has-been. No matter how busy we may become in ministry, inadequate prayer and spiritual renewal will lead to depletion of the anointing. The input is not balanced with the output.

God dependency

For the most part, it seems that much of the American Church is following the American culture. The culture is practicing self-dependency which comes natural for them as they follow the spirit of the age. A very dangerous path, rather than the biblical God-dependency which is God's will for His church. Many local churches operate on the same level of dependency as the culture [in the flesh]. Much of our church work and work of the church is done with little or no God-consciousness. We must cultivate a new:

- God-dependency
- God-consciousness
- God-anointing
- God-involvement in our ministries
- God-influences and enablement
- God must be our all-in-all

Like the apostle Paul we must be ever conscious of our total dependence upon the anointing power of God. We know that His power must saturate our total being [spirit, soul, and body]. Paul testified that his ministry was based on two things:

1. God's grace
2. God's power

He admonishes, "I became a servant of the gospel by the gift of God's grace given me through the working of His power" (Ephesians 3:7).

Both Paul's call to the ministry and his continuing daily ministry through God's anointing and enablement: *"which so powerfully works in me"* (Colossians 1:29). To him it would have been unthinkable to work for God without that power of Holy Spirit. He could do for God only as God did in and through him.

Only voluntary biblical and spiritual ignorance would allow the foolish thinking that training, skill, and experience can substitute for God's anointing and power!

The anointing has become a nominal experience for many Christians today, as have many of God's graces. This holds true even among, preachers, teachers, and many in other areas of Church leadership. Sadly, in many places so little emphasis is placed upon God's anointing to the point the people are experiencing so little faith that they have no idea what a difference the anointing makes. As a pastor, teacher and author I don't see how I or anyone else can effectively prepare or successfully minister the gifts and graces of God without the anointing. I seek a fresh anointing for everything!

Oh, my brothers and my sisters! We need a fresh anointing of the Spirit upon us. In the meantime, hold steady and pray; labor on in total dependence on God's power even when you cannot see or feel it at work. As certainly as you have experienced God's presence and anointing in the past; so certainly, you will be blessed with His presence and anointing again!

Remember God saved you

Remember you have been saved to do good works, which God has prepared in advance for you to do (Ephesians 2:10). Pray and ask God to unfold His plan for your life:

- Ask God to bring you into fellowship with other believers who love Him and have a burning desire to serve Him and reach the world.
- Ask the Holy Spirit to show you what is on His heart.
- As God shares His heart be obedient and do whatever He tells you and go wherever He sends you.
- Don't put conditions on God.
- Many refuse to corporate with God if what He wants them to do does not meet their personal criteria.
- Some people are so bold in their plans that if God tells them to go somewhere but if the dates conflict with their schedule – they may argue with the Lord that He must have missed it. God forbid!
- Followers have no right to put any conditions on God. "You are not your own; you were bought with a price. Therefore, honor God with your body" (1 Corinthians 6:19-20).

Does your life really belong to God? Is He the Lord of your life, or are you still trying to be in control, and fitting God into your busy schedule? Our work for the Lord must be the result of an overflow of our relationship with Him. Jesus is worth giving your very best service to. He willingly died for you and me. Are we willing to obey the Great Commission in return?

These are trying times; however, there is no time to waste. Our days on the earth are precious. It's time for us to renew our obedience and commitment to fulfilling our Lord's Great Commission; which is just as valid today as it was to the early church. Within each new group of students entering the Bread of Life Bible Institute, the number is increasing of those who admit that their church is not teaching, nor do they show any significant commitment to the Great Commission, other than the Sunday morning "Invitation to Discipleship" on the Church bulletin.

Building a Gospel-centered community

I am constantly surprised by the shallow gospel many pastors have built into the hearts and minds of their people. This is reflected as such a ministry structure when there is a higher priority to a church program over deep relationships. For many there is more time spent branding their programs than training small group leaders. Though we may be promoting a righteous desire for people to immerse themselves in the deep waters of biblical community, all we have to put them in is a shallow puddle from a local thunderstorm.

It's not that the people are not willing to go deeper, but the problem really lies mostly in shallow leadership. As pastors we have the responsibility to shepherd our people toward a deeper relationship and maturity in Christ. Our ability to do this may exceed our understanding of the gospel. A church where the gospel is stagnant, is like a stagnant pond with no outlet; it will always have a stench from dying things. In the case of a local church; where the gospel is static – there is no source for continuing life.

The gospel means that you and I have been set free from the bondage of Satan, sin, and death and brought into the glorious light of Christ. Our lives prior to Christ no longer defines us because we have a great story to tell. The gospel-centered community happens when we face the reality that our life is not our own, but we are bought with a price. The grace that purchased us was not cheap. The gospel is not stagnant, but continuously flows. Therefore, we are to be saturated [to overflow] with the gospel of Jesus Christ! Notice the Scripture says,

From now on, therefore, we regard no one according to the flesh. Even though we once regarded Christ according to the flesh, we regard him thus no longer. Therefore, if anyone is in Christ, he [or she] is a new creation. The old has passed away; behold, the new has come. All this is from God, who through Christ reconciled us to himself and gave us the ministry of reconciliation; that is, in Christ God was reconciling the world to himself, not counting their trespasses against them, and entrusting to us the message of reconciliation. Therefore, we are ambassadors for Christ. God is making his appeal through us. We implore you on behalf of Christ, be reconciled to God. For our sake he made him to be sin who knew no sin, so that in him we might become the righteousness of God (2 Corinthians 5:16-21 NKJV). Bracket added.

The gospel comes in and reconciles us to God – but the gospel also goes out as we become ministers of reconciliation. When the gospel isn't expressed in and through our lives the message of redemption stops in us, and creates a vacuum in our life. When we don't understand the fluid nature of the gospel – we are led to a stagnant, pseudo Christianity. When the gospel does not flow in and throughout your church, the people will be vulnerable to secular humanism, NewAge, and other false teachings and influences from the secular society around them – and away from the goal of becoming Christ-like.

A counter-cultural

A gospel-centered church (community), a living spiritual organism, is counter-cultural to today's secular society of celebrated attendance and little involvement. As stated throughout this book, the counter involves mutual:

- Love
- Care
- Commitment
- Dedication
- Authenticity

Here we seek to love the person and work of Jesus Christ in all of our lives to the glory of God. Human beings were created in the image of God who has eternally existed in community, and because of this reality, we were created for community. Though somewhat marred by sin, man is conscious of God's existence, power, and divine nature through *general revelation:* the four seasons, the rising and setting of the sun, man's depravity. Man's chief end is to glorify God – which means he is to honor Him, to acknowledge His attributes, and to praise Him for His perfections. It is to recognize His glory and worship and praise Him for it.

> *He has shown you, O man, what*
> *is good;*
> *And what does the Lord require of*
> *you*
> *But to do justly,*

> *To love mercy,*
> *And to walk humbly with your*
> *God?*
> *Micah 6:8*

Today spiritual blindness is leading many Christians corporately and individually to offer everything except the one thing He wants. Failing to give God glory is man's greatest affront to his Creator. It has been said, "Once a church moves away from these elements – we have moved away from gospel-centered community to the social club circuit.

The power of community

Christianity is always personal, for God saves people one at a time. In the first church each person expressed their personal faith and was accountable to God. However, it was not the individuals through which Christianity spread per se; it spread through the churches. As stated throughout this book, God's plan has always been community – the Body of Christ.

QUESTIONS FOR DISCUSSION & REFLECTION: CHAPTER 10

1. Discuss the variables that determine the degree of anointing the Christian receives.
2. Today many people in the local churches are content to live and minister at a mostly human level without the anointing. Why?
3. God desires that we learn to depend on His added enabling, presence, and power.
4. Contrast the weakness of striving to live by self-dependency over God-dependency.
5. We know that God's power must saturate our total being for effective life and ministry.

CHAPTER ELEVEN

GOD LOVED US FIRST

"For God so loved the world that He gave His only begotten Son, that whoever believes in Him should not perish but have everlasting life" (John 3:16).

John 3:16 is often referred to as "the Gospel in a nutshell." If the world would just hear, believe, and receive it; there is enough Gospel in v. 16 to save everyone! Nichodemus probably thought that the Messiah would come only to Israel and the benefit of His coming would be enjoyed by the Jews only; but Jesus made clear to all that God loves the entire world – Jew, Gentile, rich, poor, and bond or free, every creed and color, without exception.

Jesus Christ, the only begotten Son of God is God's gift to Adam's entire family! He came to reclaim all that the first Adam lost. There is no more wonderful announcement in all the Word of God than what we read in this verse. The devil has tried through the centuries to convince some groups that "Christianity is not for them:

- accusing God for their plight
- using economics,

- education,
- racial prejudices,
- or other variables.

Sometimes he has been able to pull it off, but today most people in America of all races and religions can read and or hear the truth; there is no excuse – that lie should not be able to keep anyone away today!

The price of redemption

God is love and pure righteousness; yet He could love a world that hated Him and hated His Son – and demanded the *death* of His Son, beat Him, nailed Him to a cross, and mocked Him while He died. He also provided salvation at the greatest cost; there is no way to even try to estimate it. God could not send angels, or any other heavenly creature to pay the price of redemption. He gave His only begotten Son. There was no other way!

Praise God! The sacrificial death of Christ has opened the door for *"whosoever will"* to come and drink of the water of life freely. Whosoever in the world believes in God's Son "shall not come into condemnation but is passed from death to life."

The love of God for the world certainly clears Almighty God of any injustice and respect of persons in judging the world by Jesus Christ. "Wherefore God also has highly exalted Him and given Him a name above every name; that at the name of Jesus every knee should bow, of things in heaven, and things in earth, and things under the earth, and that every tongue should confess that Jesus Christ is Lord, to the glory of God the Father" (Philippians 2:9-11).

He that believes not

He who believes not is condemned already *"Because he has not believed in the name of the only begotten Son of God."* Please notice, here is divine proof that there is no sin as great and damning as the *sin of unbelief.* We come down hard on people who commit adultery, idolatry, cohabitation, homosexuality, lesbianism, permissiveness, drunkenness, drugs, lying, stealing, murder and many other gross sins – but all of these are simply *fruit of unbelief!*

We find an example in Eve, who once having been deceived by Satan fell into unbelief and began to change the Word of God. She added some words and subtracted some (see Genesis 3:1-4).

It takes only ONE SIN – the sin of unbelief – to damn the soul to hell!

The person who *refuses to believe on Jesus,* unless they repent he or she is condemned already (see John 3:18). More and more people don't want to hear anything about unbelief, especially in sermons. Once deceived by Satan many people preferably select their own sin; then after looking at others, conclude they are not so bad.

They claim to be on their way to heaven anyhow. The most despicable offense to a holy God is for any man or woman to reject the glorious gift of salvation which was provided at the unknowable cost of the life of God's only begotten Son.

When we were His enemies

"But God demonstrates His own love toward us, in that while we were still sinners, Christ died for us" (Romans 5:8).

It bears repeating, the Great God of heaven, because of His great love for His enemies, gave His only begotten Son to die for His enemies. Think about that, while we were floundering impotently in the sea of our sin and our reliance on our own efforts, Christ came to our rescue!

When sinners were *"yet without strength"* in the condition in which they were powerless for good – Christ died for them. What people can just scarcely do for the good – God has done abundantly, willingly, and lovingly for the vilest of humanity!

The event of Christ's death was in no way an accident of history, but it was a purposeful act of God; therefore, the inferences we gather are exceptionally important:

- By His death Christ did for us what we would never have been able to do for ourselves. Consequently, we see in His Cross the manifestation of a goodness which transcends human standards.

- If His death declares a love that is more than human, we can only affirm that this is a manifestation of what the love of God must be.
- The strength of this passage lies in the simple values we see in a concrete life with the truth; which we conclude regards ultimate reality.
- Reconciliation is seen as dependent on the amazing goodness of God as this is manifested to us in Christ and especially as it is so supremely set forth in the Cross. This is the foundation of our spiritual conviction (see Ephesians 2:13).
- The problem that Christ's death deals with is our *failure* – our sin and alienation from God which it creates. The object which Christ's death produced is the sanctification of believers – we are now enabled to live a new righteous and victorious life.
- What Paul declares to be God's nature corresponds exactly with what Jesus teaches regarding His Father. God showed His love, said Paul, while we were yet sinners; He is kind, even to the ungrateful and the evil. Even the unjust are not beyond His reach. And what Jesus taught by word of mouth, He demonstrated by His conduct.
- While men and women were yet sinners they learned that they could come to Him, and in coming they found forgiveness and new life. The tax collectors and prostitutes heard that they had a better chance of entering God's kingdom than some whose respectability was above reproach. The good news was clear because they heard it from one who taught them by never-failing friendship and compassion; that is what restoration really means.

Our new standing and our new life

In Romans 5:9-11, Paul has shown that believers don't need to stand any longer defeated and condemned before God. They have been justified and this is the beginning of a new life.

Our new standing – Justified

The decisive step of justification was taken when our fundamental alienation was removed. If that was possible, there is absolutely nothing we need to dismiss as beyond the power of God. So, Paul is arguing from the greater objective to the less – from the fact of justification to the assurance of an abundant life (see Romans 3:21-31).

Paul never suggests that he is describing a vague or indecisive form of divine activity. Not by such means can the problem of sin be solved. *We are now,* he says, *"justified by His [Christ's] blood."* The sacrificial overtones of his statement are obvious, but now he is intent on emphasizing the fact that this is a divine activity which he is describing. God has acted decisively for our deliverance.

Unless much more were intended, God would not have done this much. He would not have brought us to a new status – especially at so great a cost – unless he intended to complete the process and bring us into fuller fellowship with Himself. We shall be saved ...... from the wrath of God.

God's reconciliation

Reconciliation is one of the great terms in the believer's vocabulary, but like so many words the misuse has made its truth unfamiliar consequently to many of our people. One of the top priorities in our local churches today should be to ensure that Christians once again master the elements of the language of our faith, and the word "reconciliation" should be a priority.

Few words deserve more careful study than this one (see v. 10; II Corinthians 5:19-20; Ephesians 2:11-17; Colossians 1:19-22). Please note five important points:

- Reconciliation is the act of God. He takes the initiative; and He works it to an appointed end. It deals with hostility so deep and settled that it would persist indefinitely unless drastic action is taken. Our situation proves that only God can solve such a grave and spiritual problem; the gospel declares that He has done so. God has acted; reconciliation is His work!
- God's reconciliation has as its main object humanity. It is for the man or woman who has rebelled against God, defied the divine purpose for his or her life, and destroyed the fellowship for which they were intended.

- Reconciliation declares that men and women who were hostile and alienated are no longer so. But it goes even further. As the passage in Colossians 1 shows conclusively – reconciliation means that our enmity to God has been replaced by the closest kind of fellowship [koinonia].
- Much more now that we are reconciled to God through the death of His Son, much more, having been reconciled, we shall be saved by His life (see Romans 5:10).
- Paul's personal understanding of reconciliation is a high mark in every passage in which he discusses the subject. What Christ has done by His death is to make *"peace through the blood of His cross"* (see Colossians 1:20).
- There is the most intimate connection between our experience of reconciliation and the fact of Christ's death and resurrection. Christ's death gave full and final expression to all those truths which a person's mind must grasp before God's mercy can come home to them.

The joy of the redeemed

Paul has just spoken of the rich life of fellowship with God to which reconciliation opens the door. It is natural that he or she should experience the exultant quality of joy which accompanies the new life. It was this quality in the early Christians that impressed and puzzled their pagan neighbors. It was very different from anything that marked ordinary human life (see v. 11).

Pleasure is one thing; joy another. Pleasure usually awakens for the moment by some outside stimulus. Joy has an enduring quality it is a state sustained by abiding sources of spiritual renewal and "no man takes" it from us. Joy is the emotional experience which God has attached to the reception of the true spiritual life for which we were created. This means it is inseparable from our proper relationship with God. In total dependence on Him and through the power of the Holy Spirit we master the disciplines of humble and happy service.

That is why we "rejoice in God." The true Christian is persuaded that there is no way of attaining the requisite fellowship with God except through Jesus Christ. The religious man or woman may speak something different. Apart from Christ we lack the knowledge of God which enables us to "exult." He has not only shown us the Father, but He has made possible the reconciliation without which there can be no joy! Give Him praise and glory!

Sin in light of Grace

Paul uses sin throughout this passage as an opponent for grace. When considered in isolation, sin produces an unwholesome preoccupation with our shortcomings. It creates a false kind of pessimistic self-condemnation or sin-consciousness, having the belief that sin is more powerful than good. It hides the important fact that the gospel does not declare that we are sinful – because that is a fact we already know (Romans 3:23).

The Gospel is *good news – not bad news!* Many things that isn't "Good News" is being promoted as "the Gospel." For instance, many Christians associate the gospel with, "You are a sinner! If you don't repent, you are going to wake up in hell!" Is that good news? True there is a heaven and a hell – and you will go to hell if you don't repent and receive salvation. Preaching on hell and scaring people to death is not preaching the gospel. Paul taught just the opposite in Romans. Instead the gospel offers *forgiveness* and *restitution* to those who have sinned (see Romans 2:4). The good news is that Jesus came and bore all our sins for us. We don't have to atone for our own sins.

The wages of sin are death; but the gift of God is eternal life through Jesus Christ our Lord (Romans 6:23).

We don't have to perform and become holy enough to earn salvation – it's a gift from God! There is a place for preaching hell, fire, and damnation; however, the true gospel specifically speaks to how we are saved. We're saved by faith in what Jesus did for us – not by faith in what we do for Him. The gospel is God's "free gift" of eternal life through Jesus Christ our Lord:

- The good news is that God doesn't want to send anyone to hell.
- You don't have to go through a great amount of religious instruction or observances – it's a gift!
- God doesn't just save the "good" people – but He justifies [extends salvation to] the ungodly (Romans 4:5).

- All you must do is believe, repent, and receive it. Believe what Jesus has done through His death, burial, and resurrection and receive eternal life and cleansing from all your sin. That is the true Gospel!

There is an anti-Gospel

There is an anti or false Gospel that believes you must do works righteousness to be "holy." Man's concepts such as: 1) right standing with God and blessings come through our own goodness and works, 2) you must come to church, 3) you must pay your tithes; and if you do these things, then God will accept you. None of this is God ordained, it is anti-gospel!

We can conclude then, if "sin" is not closely related to our thoughts of God – it subtly ceases to be "sin," and people soon *deceive* themselves that it really does not matter:

- Many people attend church each Sunday not giving any thought that they need salvation. In fact, this may account for the growing acceptance of universalism in the church today – that believes all will be saved.
- To the adherents of this view there is really no need for preaching the true gospel. God forbid! Of course, all the blame cannot be laid at the feet of the attendees.

Many churches are not presenting the pure Gospel of Jesus Christ which the apostle Paul preached – "The "power of God unto salvation" (Romans 1:16).

"There is nothing on the earth more important than having our lives; and the lives of all we meet transformed by the power of the gospel of God, which brings salvation to our souls and assures us of a home in heaven." --- Martin Luther

---

It seems that the loss of the practical foundation of *all* preaching, [the gospel of Christ], has now been specialized with its own ethics, like other professions such as politics, medicine, law, sports, banking and religion.

Therefore, the focus of the pure gospel is overshadowed in a great portion of all traditional denominations:

- From a post-Christendom point of view, never have denominations ever mattered *less*. Most people are now viewing them as relics of the *institutionalization* of the church. People don't know the fine points of doctrine, and for the most part they don't care.
- In centuries past people died for the stand they took on, for example, believer's baptism and the Lord's Supper. Today, people can think, question and argue doctrine with greater freedom, even when their total focus is "another gospel" (Galatians 1:6-7).

Denominations have been more than a doctrinal corporative. They have provided levels of authority for getting things done; and in some cases to oversee the church's identity and maintain discipline over the work (of a region). Certainly, they've provided study materials, leadership training, Christian education, and many other needful things that a *small church* could never have accomplished otherwise. Church history shows that denominations have been used of God, and will no doubt continue in one form or another.

New Realities – New Strategies

Today individual churches and leaders must learn to understand the *new realities of our culture* – so must denominations and para-church ministries. Our major denominations were built for by-gone years; which they served very well. However, they must now be rethought, because the world they were formed in years ago, no longer exists. Therefore, their systems and strategies can no longer be taken for granted. The total focus of many churches and parachurch ministries is no longer concerned with denominational beliefs and traditional identities in their names – after having made a profession of faith. Aimlessly, without a foundation of faith, they are led away from the one and only true gospel of Christ (1 Corinthians 15:1-4) to other false gospels (Galatians 1:6):

- hyper-grace gospel
- prosperity gospel
- a healing gospel
- health and wealth gospel

- name it and claim it gospel
- political gospel
- entertainment gospel
- musical gospel
- happy church gospel
- universal gospel
- no hell gospel
- support my ministry gospel

The Hyper-grace teaching [a repackaged "once saved always saved" teaching]; which claims that believers do not need to confess their sins to God. Any apostate teaching which ignores the fact of sin is deficient in its understanding of both righteousness and mercy.

That's basically the anti-gospel that religion preaches today. They may even talk about the One true God and may even mention that Jesus is the Savior of the world who died for our sins, but at its center is "another gospel" which is not the true gospel. They didn't totally deny the foundational truths of the gospel. They just perverted it and tried to add to it. Galatians was written for the same reason as Romans – to establish the grace of God. Paul also uses the *gospel* and *grace* interchangeably in Galatians. Notice how "the grace of Christ" clearly implies the Gospel:

I marvel that you are so soon removed from him that called you into the grace of God unto another gospel (Galatians 1:6).

The Gospel emphasizes God's only answer to sin – Jesus! Again, the Gospel is good news:

- It specifically refers to what Jesus did for us.
- It is based upon His performance, nor ours.
- Our good works and holiness do not earn us salvation.
- We must dispense with this dependency on "self."
- Sadly, much of what is called the Gospel today is actually promoting trust in self rather than trust in Jesus Christ, our Savior.

Paul neither minimizes nor exaggerates the gravity of sin. It is serious both because of its inherent nature and its wide dispersal. He regards it as a universal element in the human experience. All men have sinned, he says sharply; and he is simply repeating what he said previously, *"All have sinned and come short of the glory of God"* (Romans 3:23).

From his own experience, Paul knew how urgently the Gentile world needed moral regeneration. He states his conclusion from facts he determines to be incontestable. As the present section proves – he does not think of sin as transgression of a law, even one divine in origin. Coming *"short of the glory of God"* meant descending to a lower level than the one on which the human found true self-realization. The man or woman sinned and was *"alienated from the life of God"* (see Ephesians 4:18).

Sin then, was serious in its nature, universal in its extension, and disastrous in its results!

Sin after salvation

Probably one of the most unstated thoughts among church folk is, I'm not perfect, "but I'm not as bad as this brother or sister sitting on the pew next to me." This mindset of the devil always stops short of confessing; in fact, it would ignore the feelings of guilt rather than admit them:

- Only open confession of our sins will completely cleanse us.
- Only when we admit our unworthiness of God's grace can we begin a fresh start. The Scripture says,

If we say that we have no sin, we deceive ourselves, and the truth is not in us.' If we confess our sins, He is faithful and just to forgive us our sins and to cleanse us from all unrighteousness. If we say that we have not sinned, we make Him a liar, and His Word is not in us" (1 John 1:8-10).

Christians do sin, but that does not mean they have to be saved all over again. Sin in the life of a believer breaks the fellowship but does not destroy the sonship. Though he or she may not be acceptable, the true Christian is always accepted. How does God provide for the sins of the saints?

Christ's heavenly ministry

The Bible says Christ is our Advocate. The word "advocate" means "one who pleads a case" and is the same Greek word a "Comforter" in John 14:16. Through the heavenly ministry of Christ:

- We are saved from the *penalty* of sin by His death on the cross (Romans 5:6-9).
- We are saved daily from the *power* of sin (Romans 5:10).
- The Holy Spirit is Christ's representative to us on the earth, while as stated Christ, the Son, represents us to God in heaven.
- His wounds testify that He died for us – and therefore God can forgive us *when* we confess our sins.

The word "confess" "means to say the same thing." To confess sin means to say the same thing about it that God says.

Christians do not have to do penance, make sacrifices, or punish themselves when they have sinned.

God's everlasting love

It was our own sinfulness that had trapped and condemned us – yet God, out of His infinite love and mercy, chooses to save us. Since Christ had fully justified us and is presently interceding for us, then no one can possibly condemn us. Paul explains:

"What then shall we say to these things? If God is for us, who can be against us? He who did not spare His Own Son, delivered Him up for us all, how shall He not with Him also freely give us all things? Who shall bring a charge to God's elect? It is God who justifies. Who is he that condemns? It is Christ who died, and furthermore is also risen, who is even at the right hand of God, who also makes intercession for us" (Romans 8:31-34).

How can anything be added to these verses? God who is rich in mercy, spared nothing in providing salvation to humanity. Heaven was emptied of God's best to provide our redemption; He spared not His own Son – the infinite price for our redemption.

It would be strange if God should withdraw His power and leave us to the mercy of the devil, after He spared not His Son – but delivered Him up to the cross for us all. Would you think that He would leave us to the mercy of the devil after paying such a tremendous price for our salvation? The Father, after bestowing His own Son *will not* without the rest. All other gifts are small in comparison with the Gift of gifts.

But, praise God! – They are virtually included in it:

- In Christ ALL things are ours, for we are His, and He is God's (I Corinthians 3:21-23).
- All that I need is in Jesus.
- In Him I am more than a conqueror.
- We may boldly say, "God is my helper."

All my needs are supplied in Jesus; physical, spiritual, financial, mental – all needs are found supplied in Him! When the Christian comes to truly understand God's provision for a life of holiness he or she does not want to deliberately disobey Him.

QUESTIONS FOR DISCUSSION & REFLECTION: CHAPTER 11

1. Jesus Christ, the only begotten Son of God is God's gift to Adam's entire family. He came to reclaim all that the first Adam lost.
2. God could not send an angel or any other heavenly creature to pay the price of redemption. He gave His only begotten Son – there is no other way!
3. The most despicable offense to a holy God is for any person to reject His Son.
4. Reconciliation is seen as dependence on the amazing goodness of God as manifested to us in Jesus Christ especially as so supremely set forth in the Cross.
5. Joy has an enduring quality sustained by abiding sources of spiritual renewal.

CHAPTER TWELVE

OUR WALK WITH OTHERS

"A new commandment I give to you, that you love one another; even as I have loved you, that you also love one another. By this all men will know that you are My disciples, if you have love for one another" (John 13:34-35).

An important observation about walking in fellowship with Christ, which has not been mentioned yet, is that we do not walk alone. Others walk with us. Of course, there is the Lord Jesus. But there are other pilgrims too. The rule of the road is that fellowship with them is as important as fellowship with Christ Himself. Certainly, the two are intimately connected.

Our relationship with our brethren and our relationship with God are so linked that we cannot disturb one without disturbing the other. Everything that comes between us and another, such as jealousy, envy, resentment or the like, comes between us and God also.

These barriers are like thin *veils* through which we can still see, to some extent. However, if not removed immediately, they thicken into heavy curtains, and then solidify becoming as solid walls – and we are shut off from both God, our brethren, and soon shut in to ourselves. It is quite clear why these two relationships should be linked. "God is love" that is, love for others, and *the moment we fail in our love toward another, we put ourselves out of fellowship with God* – for God loves him or her even if we don't!

We are not saved to sit idly by as pew sitters – just in the number. We are saved to demonstrate love and to serve. Our love and service to God challenges us to offer our best and in turn help make the world a better place. In other words, we are called not only to make a difference in the world, but also to be the difference that the world needs (see Romans 5:5).

A walk in darkness

He calls us to demonstrate a true life of righteousness in the midst of the stark contrast of unrighteousness and even worse – the imitation of righteousness is being performed daily by many professing Christians today.

The change we make in the world is measured by the change we first make in our hearts!

Unless we are sold out to Christ in our hearts; the effects of the sin discussed above are always there to make us "walk in darkness" – that is, to cover it up and hide what we really are or what we are really *feeling*. That is always the meaning of "darkness" in Scripture, for while the light *reveals,* the darkness *hides.* The first effect of sin in us then, is to make us hide; with the results:

- That we are pretending, wearing a mask.
- We are not real with either God or man.
- Neither God nor man can have fellowship with an *unreal* person.
- Sadly, many who are in darkness have been deceived by Satan into thinking they are in the light.

The way back

The way back into fellowship with the Lord Jesus will bring us again into fellowship with our brother or sister also. All *un-love* must be recognized as sin and given to the Lord Jesus' cleansing blood; and then it can be made right with our brother or sister also. As we come back to the Lord in this manner, we find His love for our brother or sister filling our hearts and wanting to express itself in our actions toward them – and we shall walk in fellowship together again.

Only as we grow in our love for God, are we able to express His love to others!

This is the spiritual and sanctified life. It is a life to live day by day in whatever circumstances the Lord has put us. You and I are walking in complete oneness with the Lord Jesus and one another with cups continuously overflowing to the glory of God. We are in the world, but not of the world; we are called to be different. We are to live a life consistent with the Gospel of Jesus Christ rather than conform to the world's so-called social norms.

Restoring true Koinonia

Great damage is being done in the local churches by Christians who have determined that the works of the flesh [listed in an earlier chapter] including envy, strife, jealousy and the like should be treated as normal behavior then, when they attempt to carry out the mission and purpose of the church with great zeal they lack true godly love [agape] and true koinonia in their hearts.

Burdened with much access baggage in their own lives; these Christians often introduce unhealthy and unrecognized apostate teachings and secular resources that bring error into the walk and talk of weaker Christians and new converts.

What is terribly lacking in such churches is the experience of what the old church used to call "Christian love" [*agape*] and "fellowship" [*koinonia*] in the Greek – which are essential qualities of organism [body life]. Loving, welcoming, reconciling, accountable, joyous fellowship is a foundation for other church activities (Colossians 3:14). The essence of the *gospel* is uniquely embodied in the way members of a congregation treat one another. As we gathered from an earlier section, we can have no fellowship with Jesus Christ without proper fellowship with our Christian brethren and visa versa.

There are two well-known passages concerning these Spirit-filled believers in the first Church of Pentecost; as they properly managed their material resources by "sharing all things in common" (Acts 2:43-47; 4:32-35).

The sudden influx of three thousand converts ["who devoted themselves to the apostles' teaching and fellowship *"koinonia"* to the breaking of bread and the prayers] (see v. 42). Undoubtedly the community made a Spirit guided plan to meet the increased needs. The Scripture reported, *"there was not a needy person among them"* (4:34).

The word *koinonia* in verse 42 refers to the common life; the fellowship and unity characteristic of the community. According to Luke this common fellowship was experienced by the sharing of possession:

"And all who believed were together and had all things common and they sold their property and goods and distributed to all, as any had need" (vv. 44-45).

The funds from the liquidated property were laid "at the apostles' feet" (v. 35). Therefore, the church must work to restore that true "koinonia." We can glean four important qualities from them:

1. They were spirit-filled (Acts 1:8).
2. Distribution "was made to each as any had need" (vv. 34, 35).
3. The community also adhered to a promise made in Hebrew Scripture, "There will be no poor among you" (Deuteronomy 15:4).
4. The Greek ideal is recalled, "those who believed were of *one heart and soul"* (v. 32).

It is imperative that the local churches restore biblical fellowship by restoring the practice of "one another" ministry:

It is the *experience* of biblical truth that deepens our relationships with God and one another!

The inspired writers of the New Testament put great emphasis on the essentiality for Christians to know "one another" closely and intimately enough to be able to bear one another's burdens, confess faults to one another, encourage, exhort, and speak the truth in love to one another. This new emphasis on the church rather than on the family as the primary essence of community is scattered throughout the New Testament. Many statements imply, others directly teach, that it is in relationships – in groups, families, ministry teams, friendships and the like that the faith is learned, practiced, and witnessed by the world.

In addition, Christians look forward to ministering to one another with the Word, song, and prayer (in unity). There are some fifty "one another" ministry statements and commands in the New Testament which call us to this special life of love and fellowship together. Truly here is the opportunity for all Christians to live a righteous life wherein every act is worship to our God. The pagan exclaimed of the early church, "Oh! How they love one another!" The "one another" statements listed below are from the (NIV Bible):

- "Be at peace with each other" (Mark 9:50).
- "Wash one another's feet" (John 13:14).
- "Love one another" (John 18:34).
- "Love one another" (John 13:35).
- "Love one another" (John 15:12).
- "Be devoted to one another in brotherly love" (Romans 12:10).
- "Honor one another above yourselves" (Romans 12:10).
- "Live in harmony with one another" (Romans 12:16).
- "Love one another" (Romans 13:8).
- "Stop passing judgment on one another" (Romans 14:13).
- "Accept one another then, just as Christ accepted you" (Romans 15:7).
- "Instruct one another" (Romans 15:14).
- "Greet one another with a "holy kiss" (1 Corinthians 16:16).
- "When you come together to eat, wait for one another" (1 Corinthians 11:33).

- "Have equal concern for one another" (1 Corinthians 12:25).
- "Greet one another with a holy kiss" (1 Corinthians 16:20).
- "Greet one another with a holy kiss" ((2 Corinthians 13:12).
- "Serve one another in love" (Galatians 5:18).
- "If you keep on biting and devouring one another …. You will be destroyed by each other" (Galatians 5:10).
- "Let us not become conceited, provoking and envying one another" (Galatians 5:26).
- "Carry one another's burden" (Galatians 6:2).
- "Be patient with one another in love" (Ephesians 4:2).
- "Be kind and compassionate to one another" (Ephesians 4:32).
- "Forgiving one another" (Ephesians 4:32).
- "Speak to one another with psalms, hymns, and spiritual songs" (Ephesians 5:19).
- "Submit to one another out of reverence for Christ" (Ephesians 5:21).
- "In humility consider others better than yourselves" (Philippians 2:3).
- "Do not lie to one another" (Colossians 3:9).
- "Bear with one another" (Colossians 3:13).
- "Teach one another" (Colossians 3:16).
- "Admonish one another" (Colossians 3:16).
- "Make your love increase and overflow for one another" (1 Thessalonians 3:12).
- "Love one another" (1 Thessalonians 4:9).
- "Encourage one another" (1 Thessalonians 4:18).
- "Encourage one another" (1 Thessalonians 5:11).
- "Build one another up" (1 Thessalonians 5:11).
- "Encourage one another daily" ((Hebrews 3:13).
- "Spur one another on toward love and goods deeds" (Hebrews 10:24).
- "Encourage one another" (Hebrews 10:25).
- "Do not slander one another" (James 4:11).
- "Don't grumble against one another" (James 5:9).
- "Confess your sins to one another" (James 5:16).
- "Pray for one another" (James 5:16).
- "Love one another deeply from the heart" (1 Peter 1:22).
- "Live in harmony with one another" (1 Peter 3:8).
- "Love one another deeply" (1 Peter 4:8).
- "Offer hospitality to one another without grumbling" (1 Peter 4:9).

- "Each one should use whatever gift he or she has received to serve one another" (1 Peter 4:10).
- "Clothe yourselves with humility toward one another" (1 Peter 5:5).
- "Greet one another with a holy kiss" (1 Peter 5:14).
- "Love one another" (1 John 3:11).
- "Love one another" (1 John 3:32).
- "Love one another" (1 John 4:7).
- "Love one another" (1 John 4:11).
- "Love one another" (1 John 4:12).
- "Love one another" (2 John 4:21).

These "one another ministries" are essential to the church's life and very important to God, since He speaks of them so often in His Word. In this day of acute unbelief, secularism, narcissism, "materialism" and "consumerism," it is vitally important that the first work noted in this chapter be incorporated in the initial church training for new converts.

How exciting it would be for your church, or small group to flesh out these "one another ministries" as you live the way of Jesus. Think of the differences as our families, workplaces, schools, and neighborhoods are transformed!

The early churches' two-fold witness

The early church was established by the Holy Spirit upon a two-fold witness as the means of reaching an unbelieving world. Speaking the truth (Gospel) in love:

- The *kerygma,* [proclamation: *preaching* Mark16, and *teaching* Matthew 28:19-20].
- The *koinonia,* [fellowship: *love one another* John 13:34-35].

It was the combination of the two that made the early church so powerful and effective. "In the mouth of two or three witnesses shall every word be established" (Matthew 18:16).

One of the most hopeful signs on the horizon of the church worldwide is the full mobilization of non-ordained believers.

When this kind of love, sharing, teaching and burden bearing takes place in the church, the leadership will be relieved of much of the counseling and crisis intervention that confronts them today:

1. We have got to get our people to understand that reason and the sciences are natural and therefore limited.
2. The Spirit and the Word working in tandem are always the first source for wisdom and understanding.
3. Reading and applying the Scriptures every day is the best fitness program ever!

One very alert and fit, 106-year-old lady, when asked the reason for her longevity exclaimed, "I read the Bible everyday – it renews me daily!"

Relevant ministry does not require you to be perfect!

Many spiritual, physical, emotional and even mental problems could be resolved among the saints – if caring Christians would practice their biblical responsibility by showing through authentic Christian love and concern for "one another" in the body of Christ. Christians *committed to sharing their lives with "one another in love"* have less conflicts and divisions. Such believers *experience* scriptural unity in Christ by the Holy Spirit. This is exactly what Jesus prayed for:

"May they [His followers] be brought to complete unity to let the world know that you sent me and have loved them even as you have loved me" (John 17:23). Bracket mine.

Loving unity sets believers apart in a world where envy, jealousy, and hatred characterize many relationships. Paul wrote, "God has so composed the body .... that there should be no division in the body, but that the members should have *"the same care for one another"* (1 Corinthians 12:24-25). Emphasis added.

My wife and I were in Panama in 1970-73 and had the opportunity to see what some missionaries were recieving as help from back in the States. Some local churches and ministries had become satisfied in just giving things away; in some cases, giving things that would normally be discarded. They are self-satisfied and many times that is the essence of their disunity, strife, envy and such *decreases*.

The kinds of Christians who "love one another deeply from the heart" (1 Peter 1:22) are those whom God can use to share His love with others. This, assures the willing preparation and participation of your church for living organism [body] ministry. A church's lasting impact is not only in its structured ministries of outreach but also [and sometimes *especially*] in the informal relationships and ordinary, day-to-day acts of compassion and fellowship among members. When the world observes the love, care and unity of the body of believers – they will come because their spiritual as well as their physical needs will be met! They want to hear about the source of the love that met them right at their deepest need. Hope comes from a church that reflects Jesus, one that calls forth the reaction, *"See how they love one another!"* Give Him praise and glory!

Further focus

The focus of making disciples of Jesus Christ should be based on the example of Jesus. It is very essential that we observe his character, mission, and life, encouraging one another to trust and follow Him fully being united to Christ: crucified, buried, and raised with Him, living a life that challenges societal norms, especially when those norms threaten the freedom and dignity of the most vulnerable – rather than relying on the world's deceptive systems, definitions, and processes as helpful as they may seem to be.

Research shows:

- The world's definitions can easily become judgmental and therefore hinder or deny opportunities.
- Therefore, we should strive to describe the heart, beliefs, attitudes, worldview, and activities of Christ followers, "And let us consider one another to stir up love and good works" (Hebrews 10:24).
- We are called to be like Jesus.

The Holy Spirit's work of uniting us to Christ makes us not mere imitators but living members of His body. We are incorporated, baptized, into Christ's death, burial, and resurrection. And we should never lose sight of that goal. A disciple is a follower of Jesus Christ who continuously seeks to obey His teachings, and to imitate His way of life.

"A student is not above his or her teacher, nor a servant above his or her master. It is enough for the student to be like his or her teacher, and the servant like his or her master" (Matthew 10:24-25). Paraphrase is mine. Toward the end of his life Paul wrote to Timothy:

> *All Scripture is given by inspiration of God,*
> *and is profitable for doctrine,*
> *for reproof, for correction,*
> *for instruction in righteousness,*
> *that the man of God*
> *may be complete,*
> *thoroughly equipped*
> *for every good work.* II Timothy 3:16-17

Paul admonishes believers corporately and individually to be thoroughly equipped; to display and manifest the glory of God, thus vindicating God's character against all the slander of demonic realms, that say God is not worth living for. God has entrusted to His church the glory of His name. The warmth which comes from a Christian Community joyfully singing, heartily worshipping people can melt the cold hearts which have been insulated against the Holy Spirit's influence.

QUESTIONS FOR DISCUSSION & REFLECTION: CHAPTER 12

1. Discuss the downward spiral of continuing sin in relation to our fellowship with God and the brethren.
2. Light reveals while darkness hides; therefore, the first effect of sin is to hide.
3. When Christians are committed to "one another" conflicts, and divisions decrease, and those believers experience Spiritual oneness.
4. People flock to churches that minister to their deepest needs.
5. Loving unity separates true believers in a world where the works of the flesh characterize many relationships.

ENDNOTES

INTRODUCTION

[1] Webster's New Explorer Dictionary and Thesaurus (Merriam-Webster, Inc. 1999) 616

[2] Ibid. 501 The Greek term *hierateuo* "a body of priests consisting of the *whole* church called "a holy priesthood" [not a special order from among them].

Chapter 1: Relevance a good Strategy?

[3] Ibid. 535 Note: the Greek word *hieros* "denotes consecrated to God" e.g. the Scriptures.

[4] Webster's New Explorer Dictionary – page 471: secular means not sacred or ecclesiastical. Indifference to or exclusion of religion. No God!

[5] Ibid. 179

[6] Ibid. 93

[7] Jay R. Leach, *Battle Cry* (Trafford Publishing, 2016) 24

[8] Jay R. Leach, *According to Pattern* (Trafford Publishing, 2016) 46

Chapter 3: A Divided Life

[9]   W.E. Vine's Greek Grammar and Dictionary (Thomas Nelson, 2012) 505. Note: Through the "propitiatory" sacrifice of Christ, he or she who believes in Him is by God's own act delivered from justly deserved wrath and comes under the covenant of grace.

[10]   Unger's Bible Dictionary, (Moody Press, 1974) 1159. There are several Greek terms *'arete* is the first one denoting a virtuous course of thought, feeling, and action, *moral goodness* (II Peter 1:5), and particular *moral excellence, as modesty, purity,* (Philippians 4:8). The latter term indicates *power, ability,* and is often so rendered. In Mark 5:30; Luke 6:19; 8:46, it indicates the power of Christ to heal disease. The culture has accepted that virtue is relative and therefore to them determined by popular consensus, and expressed through laws, customs, and mores.

[11]   David Augsburger, *Dissident Discipleship* (Brazos Press, 2006)

Chapter 4: Living a Double Life

[12]   Ibid. 35

[13]   Webster's New Explorer Dictionary and Thesaurus (Merriam-Webster, Inc 1999) 382

[14]   Note: I Thess, 4:17; John 14:1-3; and I Cor. 15:51, 52, together form the biblical basis for "the Rapture" of the church. After the dead come forth, their spirits, already with the Lord (2 Cor. 5:8; Phil. 1:23), are now being joined to resurrected new bodies (I Cor.15:35-50), the living Christians will be raptured, caught up, or snatched away "in the air" (John 10:28; Acts 8:39).

Chapter 6 Perilous Times

[15]   Teacher's Outline & Study Bible by Alpha-Omega Ministries, Inc. (1994) 75

[16]   A realm in which the damned will suffer everlasting punishment prepared for the devil and his cohorts and the unsaved. Webster's New Explorer Dictionary and Thesaurus (Merriam-Webster, Inc 1999) 242

Printed in the United States
By Bookmasters